Verna Marchman
November, 1970

WHERE
ARE
YOU, GOD?

David A. Ray

WHERE ARE YOU, GOD?

Fleming H. Revell Company
Old Tappan, New Jersey

To my wife Patsy, who has been a source of wonderful inspiration
for me to try to live according to
the principles outlined in this book

Contents

Introduction

God is close by, very close to you.

Through prayer, faith, openness, and dedication to God, His magnificent nearness and nowness become explosively active in you. Instead of God being *out there* somewhere, He is *right there* in life with you. Living then becomes a spring of power, courage, calmness, and confidence. I hope these pages impress you with that grand truth.

Without the encouragement of two of the great ministers of our time, Norman Vincent Peale and Charles L. Allen, I would not have undertaken to write this book.

Without the understanding of the congregation of the Valley Community Drive-In Church, San Dimas, California, I would not have had time to write this book.

Without the assistance of my loyal secretary, Frances Molsberry, I would not have been able to complete this book.

DAVID A. RAY

1.

—When I'm Lonely?

On a television program in Los Angeles, which had to do with the most annoying noises, a commentator asked a number of people what noise bothered them more than any other.

One man, apparently weary of the traffic tie-ups, said, "Freeway noise, that's undoubtedly the worst. At 5 P.M. it's the most unbearable." A woman who lives next to the International Airport answered, "Those jets taking off and landing—I don't think I can stand them any longer." It was a young man who gave the answer that interested me the most; in fact, his reply startled me. As his eyes reflected his thought, he replied, "Loneliness is the most terrible noise in my life. Yeh," he commented, "being alone. Quietness. I can't take it."

I've met a lot of lonely people. This stuffed American society has a big and growing club of them, and there are some who take advantage of people's lonely feelings.

In Los Angeles newspapers, the classified section has a long column of lonely-heart organizations.

"Lonely?" one ad begins, "Find the dream of your dreams and never be lonely again."

People aren't the whole answer, though. I have talked to loneliness-ridden people who are surrounded by others. Their lives are full of human beings yet they they are still lonely.

Another ad is directed to "Adults Without Partners." Through modern electronic devices, this group matches up individuals. It produces computerized couples on the basis of mutual likes, dislikes, education and so forth.

Similarities don't guarantee compatibility, either. I've talked to many couples and business partners who are so much alike they can hardly stand one another.

One of my closest friends confided in me that he was seriously thinking of dissolving a very successful business partnership. "What on earth would cause you to do that?" was my question.

Marvin told me that he and his partner were too much alike to continue their business together any longer, because, "Both of us are miserable with each other."

Similarities can be an asset, and so can dissimilarities. When all the facade is brushed away, they are what you make of them.

It is in our very nature not to feel lonely. We want that wholesome, belonging feeling. When we don't have it, our instincts drive us on to get it somehow and somewhere.

This is demonstrated vividly in an experience of Rupert Brooke, the English poet. At the time of his departure from Liverpool for New York, Mr. Brooke noticed that the other passengers on the ship had friends on the dock to bid them farewell. No one was there to wave good-bye to the poet and he felt very lonely and desolate. There in the distance, Mr. Brooke saw a little newspaper boy all by himself. He rushed off the ship and got hold of the boy.

"What's your name, son?" asked Mr. Brooke.

"Bill."

"Bill, do you want to earn a shilling?"

Like most boys, Bill felt this was a lot of money. He quickly nodded his head yes.

"Then," said Mr. Brooke, "stand yonder on the dock and wave goodbye to me as the boat passes by."

The great Englishman often remembered the little street lad who was the answer to his loneliness.

In my experience, I have found the most effective solution for loneliness is through another person who feels lonely. You can do more to dispel your own loneliness than anybody else. In pursuit of a new-styled you which brings the curtains down on loneliness, it is essential for you to get some points clarified. For example, you must recognize the difference between being alone and being lonely.

TO BE ALONE IS A FACT OF LOCATION, WHEREAS LONELINESS IS AN INNER FEELING OF SEPARATION.

Carl Sandburg has brightened the American literary scene with his writings and keen insight. He is the one who reminds us that Shakespeare, Leonardo da Vinci, Benjamin Franklin and Abraham Lincoln never saw a movie, nor heard a radio, nor watched television. Imagine that! They still became men of gigantic achievements, emotionally stable, mentally balanced and properly developed human beings. Almost incredible! How did those men become great? They learned the blessing of being alone; for when they were alone, the creative mood in them was let loose to do its magnificent work.

A great amount of good can be accomplished when you're alone. Many times the Galilean Master went off to be alone to pray, to meditate and think, or to get a better perspective and insight as to what He was to do with His life. In this solitude, He found strength; and in quietness, He met God.

As I write these words, I am by myself and with God in the quietness of the scenic western Tennessee farmland. Inside, I feel a productive surge amid my aloneness and the stillness of the beautiful countryside. There is a release for ideas generated in this relaxing setting.

Some California ministers were sharing methods we have discovered to work in sermon preparation and I mentioned that I keep pencil and pad in my car and especially at my bedside, for often late at night and early in the morning, there is a flow of thoughts which does not come at any other time. A colleague asked, "Why do you suppose this happens?"

My opinion is that at those times the mind is expecting quietness. Occasionally the phone does ring and emergency situations do arise, but for the most part, there are no interruptions; and the spiritual, mental and physical structure is acclimated to the opportunity. The idea center finds a chance to really activate itself. The lock is removed, the door is opened and the thoughts flow out. Solitude, quietness, and aloneness make the opportunity.

Have you found the greatness, the depth, the power, the re-creativity of being alone? According to Anne Lindbergh, we must relearn to be alone. That's wise advice for a group-conscious, pace-setting, fast-moving generation. "Loneliness is only an opportunity," said Anna Monroe, "to cut adrift and find yourself." Bruce Barton claimed, "It would do the world good if every man in it would compel himself occasionally to be absolutely alone. Most of the world's progress has come out of such loneliness."

Loneliness, however, is feeling that you're forsaken. It pries into your emotional structure. The ancient psalmist must have felt forsaken when he cried, ". . . I am like a lonely bird on the house-top" (Psalms 102:7, RSV). The troubled teen-ager felt forsaken when she sobbed, "My mother and dad don't really care about me." When you lose a loved one, you may very well feel forsaken. What causes such a feeling?

Dr. Arthur W. Combs, Professor of Psychology and Counseling at the University of Florida, claims that it is caused by a lack of fulfillment in life. Commonly, the one who has no sense of purpose and direction, or no sense of achievement, will be at odds with people and society.

Self-fulfilled people have a feeling of oneness with others, according to Dr. Combs.

A noted medical doctor, Maxwell Maltz, believes that loneliness is caused by an alienation from life; in other words, a withdrawal from living or a hibernation from life's activities. This is the old by-my-selfish attitude in workclothes. It will cause a person to deteriorate and ultimately destroy him. You can win over this attitude, even if you're by yourself.

Of all people who have been isolated by their jobs, it seems to me that the old lighthouse keepers have to rank at the top of the list. Perched on a few feet of rock, those men were encircled by an expanse of water farther than the eye could see. Talk about being lonely! A man named Dickens was one of those old sea salts.

One day he was asked about his job. "Isn't it terribly lonely out there?"

With a voice as coarse as gravel, as tough as leather and as stout as a bull, Dickens answered, "Not at all! It isn't lonely, nor is it unpleasant. My business is to keep the lights burning bright and sharp at all times. I have to keep the reflectors clear. You see, the safety of many people depends on me."

In the midst of being alone, that crusty old sailor had found an affinity with life, a great amount of pleasure and challenging activities. Loneliness couldn't touch him.

Another distinguished doctor suggests that the feeling of loneliness comes from an overprotective spirit: it's a form of self-insulation from the realities and affronts of modern living.

Says such a person, "If I don't do anything, I won't get hurt." This spirit is evidenced by a lack of drive, initiative and ambition. It is shown by pessimism and fear.

"I'm afraid to try that. Even if I do, I'll fail. When I fail, the fall will be a hard one." Like the outcome of Humpty Dumpty, this person is afraid that when he falls, he can never be put together again. That's the story of the former Mr. Cautious.

One day he heard a man say, "So, you're afraid to try. You think you'll blunder. Well, you might stub your toe, but it ought to hurt you more to go through life as a person who is scared to try." That started him thinking. Eventually, he began praying and believing and he became dynamized inside.

"I was so afraid of life," he admitted, "that I tip-toed through it so that I wouldn't ever fail. But, you know, I was a failure. I failed to live. I was so cautious, it strangled me spiritually. I actually believe today, that it is much better to go down trying to do something big than it is to succeed at being a failure." He's right!

Now, this man is a very successful businessman in West Covina, California. Life has become a swelling adventure for him. But it took some strong words to break the overcautious shell that hemmed in the man.

At the heart of feeling lonely is a form of godlessness. The lonely person feels himself minus God. He feels that God is gone, or that

15

God is removed. What can you do when you feel lonely? First, you can become involved with people and projects.

Doing things with other people and enjoying them helps us forget ourselves constructively. There is a therapeutic power which is found in projecting yourself into people-centered projects. The loneliest people usually are the most self-centered people. They direct most of their thoughts and efforts toward themselves. They have no outlets and all channels in their lives are dammed up. More often than not, they end up damming life.

"Force yourself," challenged a psychologist who is a friend of mine, "to mix and mingle with other people." Have an active, not passive, association. Get into your church, a civic organization or a neighborhood project by which you can benefit others. Become a one-man people changer. By helping to change people, you change yourself. As a friend of mine, Kenneth Thompson, put it, "You help yourself by helping others." Mr. Thompson has retired from public life after forty illustrious years as a California highway engineer, but he hasn't retired from living. He and his wife have poured themselves into projects through their church. "We're helping people, and it's helping us," they both claimed. As their minister, I know that they are changing people for the good, and they are being changed for the better.

The second way to handle loneliness constructively is to do your best honestly, to be at one with all people.

Catherine Marshall, that wonderful Christian woman and best-selling author, truthfully speaks of the Kingdom of God as the kingdom of right relationships. One of the best verses from the Bible tells us, "If possible, so far as it depends upon you, live peaceably with all" (Romans 12:18, RSV).

What happens if there is someone with whom a happy relationship seems out of the question? A very conscientious man told me that no matter what he did, he and Mr. So-and-So were at odds with one another. "We can't get along," he insisted.

"Can't!" I answered. "You mean you won't."

I encouraged the man to think well of his adversary, to speak well of him, and to go out of his way to mend broken-down relationships. The idea was that he must do his best to be at one with the man.

That word *can't* has no place in your vocabulary. What's more important, it should be thrown out of your thinking. Quit thinking *can't*. Furthermore, rub it off your personality. Junk it from your talk. It's a blinder to spiritual vision, a thorn in the flesh to personal growth and a killer of satisfactory human relationships.

When you honestly do your best to be at one with others, you are living out your Christian obligation. Simultaneously, you are opening a fresh door of happiness for you. And you can expect to have better relationships with people when you do your best. Your attitude and activity will help bring on the fact.

The third suggestion for getting free from loneliness is to separate fact from feeling.

A man came to me one day and said, "I know that people are talking about me. They're criticizing me for my stand in the board meetings."

"How do you know they're talking about you and criticizing you?" I asked.

"Well, every time I see them, they're looking at me, and when I walk over, they stop talking."

I questioned the man further. "Have you heard them criticize you? Have you asked if they are talking about you? Are you absolutely sure they were talking about you?"

To all of my questions, his answer was no. My friend needed to separate fact from feeling. He felt they were critical of him, when in fact they were admiring his fine sharkskin suits!

Keep in mind that feeling may not be substantiated by fact. You may feel forsaken, when in fact you have an army of friends around you.

"Do you feel forgiven?" someone asked Martin Luther.

"No," he answered, "but as sure as there's a God, I'm sure that I am forgiven." The reformer separated fact from feeling.

Jesus did, too. ". . . I am not alone," He said on the eve of His death, "for the Father is with me" (John 16:32 rsv). The greatest medicine for loneliness is God in you. You must believe that He is in you. Often, I suggest that people confront all doubts and

17

circumstances with the words, "[My] Father [God] is with me."
Say it audibly with me, "[My] Father [God] is with me."
Get rid of loneliness. Wash it out: you can—today!

WHAT TO DO WHEN YOU FEEL LONELY

1. Quietness can be a blessing to cure loneliness.
2. Loneliness is a feeling, and you can govern your feelings.
3. Engage your life in self-fulfilling activities.
4. Put some *dare* in your life. This will work against the over-protective spirit.
5. Do your best to maintain harmonious relationships with others and take the initiative to correct misunderstandings.
6. Know that God is by your side. His presence knocks out loneliness.
7. Repeat the Twenty-third Psalm often when you're lonely. Think about it, as you do, then say, "This means me." It really does!

2.

—When I Am Frustrated?

Examination of the realities of life reveals that if you wish to be a leader, you will be frustrated. If your aim is to be a servant, you will rarely be frustrated. Everyone, whether he is the leader or the led, will meet frustration at some time or another. Sometimes it comes on a jammed freeway at 5:00 P.M., or perhaps it happens when a wife begins to get ready at 7:30 and the engagement is set for 8 o'clock. Frustration may come when there's a deadlock on what could be the biggest sale in the company's history.

We will not live without some frustrations. We are human beings, and human beings get frustrated. Sometimes our plans and procedures fall down. When this happens, we need to make the frustration work *for* us, and we can do that. If there is no way that we can change a situation, we must accept it gracefully.

Bob Donally went to International Airport to board a jet for Houston, Texas. He was due to close a multimillion dollar oil lease arrangement. What a day it was for him! Boarding was announced, and Bob took his seat on the plane. It was 7:20 and departure was scheduled for 7:30. In two hours, he would be in Houston for the important appointment. Seven-thirty arrived. Nothing happened. At 7:35 the Captain announced a braking difficulty. Departure was reset for 8:00. At 8:10, again the Captain announced the problem was unsolved and that the flight would depart at 8:30. Another delay and a complete change of planes put departure at 10:30, and Bob's important appointment was for 10:00. Bob bowed his head and said, "Lord, there seems to be nothing I can do about this matter. I'm resigning myself to take the matter without fit or fury."

When there is nothing you can do about a matter, resign yourself to the fact. Do whatever you can to be constructive.

Many people have talked to me about their frustrations and about what they do when they get frustrated. Some of them said that what they thought would be a haven from the hard facts of frustration turned out to be an hallucination.

In frustration, it is important to build yourself up. If you determine in your mind to be victorious and happy when you're frustrated, you will put your frustrations to good use; and you will recover from your frustrations rather than be ruined by them.

When frustrated, you can receive great benefit from listening to others of faith-filled attitudes. Often, people talk as much as they do because they are insecure and scared. They aren't sure of themselves and they fear that what others say might be more important than what they have to talk about. But from a faith-thinking person, you can expect inspiration, solid ideas, enthusiasm, and understanding. Such people will enlarge your life, particularly during the rough times. Don't be afraid to listen to them.

Especially, listen to the voice of God. Be sure to get His guidance through your frustration. Jesus said, "Push the boat out further to the deep water and . . . let your nets down for a catch." "Master," Simon answered, "we worked hard all night long and caught nothing. But if you say so, I will let down the nets" (Luke 5:4-5, TEV). He was willing to listen to the voice of God through his frustration.

A man told me that he doesn't believe that God guides people today. The trouble isn't in guiding, but listening. People don't listen for God.

When you listen to Him, you'll find the creative, useful and satisfying inner stuff to handle your frustration. I'm sure you will discover that the way out of frustration is found, not by resenting it, but by capitalizing on the lessons to be learned from frustration, as it is set up in the sphere of God's purpose for you. As God sees it, frustration can be the salt of life. Is it not true at times that building can commence only after we are broken and bent?

Frustration, if you let it have its proper effect, says, "God is your greatest need." Thomas Carlyle was sitting by his fire on a cozy Sunday afternoon when someone knocked at his door. It was the young minister who had just arrived in the community. The new minister was seeking the wise advice of the great Carlyle. "Mr. Carlyle," he said, "I want to do some real and lasting good in this community. What do you think is the most important thing I can do?"

Carlyle was quiet for a moment. He leaned over to poke the fire. Then, the famous gentleman said, "What this country needs is a man who knows God other than by hearsay." Get to know God and help other people get to know Him.

There is a verse from the Bible which can help you do this. Deuteronomy 30:19-20, RSV

> . . . I have set before you life and death, . . . therefore choose life, that you and your descendants may live, . . . loving the Lord your God . . . obeying his voice, and cleaving to him; for that means life and the length of days to you. . . .

WHAT TO DO WHEN YOU ARE FRUSTRATED

1. Put frustration to work for you.
2. Accept in goodwill what you cannot change.
3. Keep doing good, even when you're frustrated.
4. Seek the help of faith-thinkers when you are frustrated.
5. Learn from your frustration the lessons that will help you live a fuller life.
6. See God through your frustration; get to know Him through it all; adjust yourself more completely to the divine purposes in life.

3.

—When My Faults Burden Me?

One of the most unusual pictures I've ever seen was a line drawing vividly depicting a modern reality. Standing erect on top of the world was a tall cross, rising majestically into the heavens. It was beautiful, giving the idea of strength and courage.

But beside the cross, pointing into a dark sky, stood an imposing missile with a nuclear warhead perched threateningly on its nose. I stared at it for several minutes, realizing that the two symbols reflect different messages. On one hand, the cross demonstrates love; on the other, the warhead demonstrates hate. Both indicate that we have faults.

A man who admitted to some faults in his life selected the following epitaph for his own grave marker: "Born—a human being; died—a wholesale grocer." He explained by saying, "I was so busy selling groceries that I didn't have time for a family. I was so busy selling groceries that I didn't have time for travel, although I had plenty of money. I was so busy selling groceries that I didn't have time for drama, lectures, concerts, reading, neighbors, mountains, lakes or streams. I was so busy selling groceries that I didn't have time for the church or for community service.

"All of these were pushed out by the grocery business. I was successful and I became a large wholesaler, but I was so busy making a living that I never had time to live." I am afraid this is a fault many hurried Americans have.

As I continued looking at the cross and the missile, a young friend called to my attention that the missile followed the cross and that the failure of the cross, and what it represents to mankind, is shown up by the missile. I'm of a different opinion.

Christianity has not failed; only men and nations. We have failed to practice the way of Jesus and that has been our fault of greatest consequence. People of all faiths admit to the peace giving power of Jesus' teaching. Admiral Richard E. Byrd declared that there would be no war in a God-directed world.

Two thousand years ago men cried out before Pilate, ". . . Not this man [Jesus], but Barabbas [a murderer and robber]!" John 18:40, RSV. Two thousand years later, men are still crying out, if not in word, then by thought and deed, ". . . Not this man, but Barabbas!" (John 18:40, RSV). Not the way of Jesus, but the way of destruction through violence, turmoil, conflict, and hatred. The British playwright, George Bernard Shaw, said that Jesus hasn't been a failure yet, for nobody has ever been sane enough to try His way.

Now, try His way and see what happens to those faults which burden you. They can be overcome by truly attuning your life to the way of Christianity. Many people have discovered this. Apply the five R system of Christianity for besting your shortcomings: recognize, record, redress, recess, and rejoice.

You can overcome your faults, but first you must recognize them. One of the smartest men ever to live was Thomas Carlyle who believed that the greatest fault is to be conscious of none.

I remember the young man who said that he was at a stalemate in life. "I'm not getting anywhere," he confessed. "and there isn't any zip to living any more." I listened to his sincere story and told him that he had already started the way out of his dilemma, because he recognized the trouble. That is a big step.

By recognizing that you have faults, you begin the climb which will lead you to overcome them. Many of us never fully see our own shortcomings. Oh, the vision is 20-20 when looking at the lives of others. Their faults are quickly recognized and expounded upon. Jesus told a story of a man like that. Two men went to the church supposedly to pray. One prayed; the other prattled. The one who prayed said, "God, be merciful to me a sinner!" (Luke 18:13, RSV), whereas the other man did nothing except point out his own mistakes by concentrating on the mistakes he saw in others.

The statesman Bernard Baruch used to say to his associates that two things are bad for the heart—running upstairs and running down people. We know that he is at least half right.

It takes humility, courage, and strength to admit that you have faults. At this point of honest recognition, the small-spirited person will be left behind, perhaps because he feels that to recognize faults is a sign of weakness.

The second R in mastering your faults is to record them on paper in the order in which you want to overcome them. This is to note them—not to make a record to be played back over and over again, but to provide a point of visual contact. Place the big ones first.

Often, in my pastoral counseling, I ask a person to write out a list of his faults. He must come to some reasonable conclusion as to what it is he is to overcome, and by recording the faults on paper, he has the opportunity to look them over.

Such a list must represent conscientious thought. It must represent honesty with yourself. Pull no punches, and face the raw truth.

After recording those faults as completely as you can, then begin to *redress*, the third R. A fault confessed is half-redressed; therefore, it is most important to recreate and rebuild yourself. There is a verse in the Bible of great help to me because it shows how to make redress for faults. "The one thing I do, however, is to forget what is behind me and do my best to reach what is ahead" (Philippians 3:13, TEV).

"I do"—two words by which you can change your life—not talk about, think about, tease about, or toss about, rather, I do.

I do *one* thing at a time. The high command of the Allied armies during World War II was faced with a momentous decision. Where would the next major front be launched? How many lines of attack should the allies have? The leading strategists were certain that only one front (well planned, well equipped, and well executed), should be attempted at a time. That's a practical lesson to learn in getting the upper hand on your shortcomings.

Choose one at a time—not many. The *many* will divert your

energy and sap all hope from you. The *many* will order division and father confusion. Select one at a time.

Do your best from now on. There is a new beginning for you. Never does anyone get to a place in life where he cannot do his best from that time on.

The fourth R, by which you can gain victory over a fault, is *recess*. You must avoid the fault psychology which comes about when a person keeps his mind filled with his errors. That is what I mean by making a record of your shortcomings. A record will be played back and you don't need a record of your shortcomings. You must not let your faults bear on your mind, and a way to keep them in their creative corner is to take a *recess* from them.

Jesus wisely advised, "Come ye yourselves apart . . ." (Mark 6:31, KJV). One minister made a very good commentary on these words when he said that Jesus meant for us to come apart or we *will* come apart.

When my wife and I go on vacation, we usually make an irrevocable agreement that we will not think or talk about our church. We love it; Christian work is my life. There is no place I would rather be than where I am, but we have found out that we must take a break from the normal routine of our work. Otherwise, we will be broken over it. Efficiency, energy and enthusiasm will be sacrificed. Insight and creative expression will be lost. A recess is a break, and to do anything constructive about your shortcomings, the principle of recess must be put into action.

Oh, what an R *rejoice* is! It produces tremendous power by which a human being can move ahead of his faults. Anyone can rejoice, for today is the Almighty's opportunity for him to do something about those nagging shortcomings. "This is the day which the Lord has made; let us rejoice and be glad in it" (Psalms 118:24, RSV). People are sapped of spiritual and physical energy by their faults because they don't take advantage of the centuries-old teaching that men can rejoice (be happy) *today*. For the first twenty years of a man's life, his parents ask where he is going. For the next thirty years, his wife asks where he is going. For the next fifteen years, his grandchildren ask where he is going, and at his funeral, his mourners ask where he is going.

I'm not of the conviction that life needs to be a rat race. As a matter of fact, I am convinced that life in you can be so wonderful that you will look forward to each dawn with the idea that something really good is going to happen to you today. Each day can be full of delight and worthwhile. If you approach every day in that spirit, you are going to win out over some faults every day; but there are three power-packed words to this rejoicing frame of mind—they are *current, creator,* and *cheerful.*

Keep *current* on your days. This is to be contemporary with your life. I met a very interesting attorney who illustrated the meaning of this. He exhibited great respect for the court system of this nation and he spoke admiringly of a certain judge, describing him as understanding, possessing unusual insight, and being very approachable. "After all," the counsel remarked, "like the rest of us, he puts on his pants one leg at a time."

The well-proven technique for a delightful day requires the philosophy of one-leg-at-a-time. Keep current on your days. "This is the day . . ." (Psalms 118:24, rsv). It *is*. It is *today*, not *days*. The emphasis is on *one* day rather than several.

When you wake up on Monday, say, "This is the *Monday* the Lord has made." On Tuesday say, "This is the *Tuesday* the Lord has made," and so on throughout the week.

Obviously, it would be ridiculous and incorrect to get up on Monday morning and say, "This is the Tuesday the Lord has made," or, "This is the Sunday the Lord has made," or, "This is the Monday and Tuesday the Lord has made." But in life and mind many people do it.

Break the duplicity of multi-day existence. There's only one way to do it. Keep current on your days.

When you keep your days current, you can claim, "This is the day which the Lord has made." (Psalms 118:24, rsv).

Among the viewers of our television worship is a voice teacher. She wrote me and offered some very sound advice. "I watch the tv worship," she said, "and each week you open with those words from Psalms. Let me suggest that you control your voice so as to emphasize the word *Lord*. That's the word in the verse to accent," she recommended. "Every other part of the statement hinges on *Lord*." If you read the Psalm, I believe you will agree.

TODAY

The Lord is good (everything He does with me is good and for my good).

God's love is steadfast (it's keeping-on love).

God is interested in my life (He is with me through distress).

The Lord sets me free (spiritually, emotionally, and physically) through prayer.

God is on my side (we are partners).

With the Lord on my side, I am not afraid.

I can win over any fault.

The Lord helps me out of tight places (Psalm 118:1, 5, 6, 7, 13, RSV).

The Psalmist would agree with the British writer, George Bernard Shaw, who said that we must beware of the man whose God is in heaven. He is busy here, too—now, today, this moment and on our behalf. There are substantial reasons to "rejoice and be glad."

Become a *cheerful* person today. "This is the day which the Lord has made . . ." (Psalms 118:24, RSV). In that case, every one of us can be full of joy and gladness. One of the strongest affirmations ever made is, "I can do all things through Christ which strengtheneth me" (Philippians 4:13, KJV). By substituting the word *be*, that affirmation becomes one of the greatest declarations for Christian personality development one can make. Read it this way. "I can be [a cheerful person today] through Christ which strengtheneth me." "I can be [a cheerful person *now*] through Christ which strengtheneth me."

A woman told me that she got to the point where she had to have three cups of coffee, three cigarettes, and fifteen minutes in the mornings before the children were allowed out of their rooms. "I was a grouch all of the time, but especially in the morning."

She discovered that she could be cheerful, and she did it by using the letters in C-H-E-E-R-F-U-L.

1. *Choose* to be cheerful.
2. *Handle* irritating people and problems with prayer and poise.
3. *Enjoy* the day by appreciating what you have.
4. *Enrich* your life by sincerely trusting God with each day.
5. *Radiate* happiness by your looks and behavior.
6. *Face* each day with *faith* that Christ and you will make it a victory.
7. *Understand* that God wants you to have a successful day. Undress the fears and worries toward the day by understanding that God and you are bigger than they are.
8. *Loose* yourself from bitterness by accepting a setback gracefully in the spirit that you are going to bounce back a better and bigger person.

Spiritually, you will find *rejoice* to be a revolutionary force to take care of your faults.

WHAT TO DO WHEN YOUR FAULTS BURDEN YOU

1. Believe that you can overcome your faults.
2. Believe that God will help you overcome them.
3. Look for ways to do it.
4. Get God's guidance through prayer.
5. Never quit in your efforts to improve.

4.

—When I'm Unhappy?

Everywhere I go, I tell people to be happy, and I try to let them know how their lives can be brimful of happiness. One of the strongest convictions I hold is that true religion makes people happy. Apply the principles of Christianity to life on a day-to-day basis, and the happiness of the ages will be yours every day.

I have in mind the experience of Johnny Bob.

Johnny Bob was a part-time box-boy who worked with me at the Butternut Street M System supermarket in Abilene, Texas. I knew this delightful human being as Mr. Happiness. We're told that teens are bored, but not that fifteen-year-old. He was always smiling, and not everything that happened to him was funny! When others complained, he poured on the good cheer. When others criticized, he spoke of the good in his job. When others loafed on the job, he worked hard. His job was a project to him. His personality was infused with joy. Life was thrilling to him.

I knew that Johnny Bob was a church-goer, but that didn't assure him happiness. There are many other church-goers who are profoundly unhappy. As for his family, he was from one on the lower end of the totem pole. Then how was he so immensely happy? I couldn't help but ask him one afternoon.

"Look," he said, "I've got a lot of work to do now. Let's talk after closing time." I had never seen such integrity, either. I could hardly wait until closing time.

"You ask me what makes me so happy," he reminded me. "Jesus Christ and His way of life that I'm learning to live." Johnny Bob, as a teen-ager, found happiness that defies description through Christianity and a daily application of its principles.

You can, too. I'm sure of it! And I have good reason—namely, because of sayings like this from the Bible:

> Behold, what I have seen to be good and to be fitting is to eat and drink and find enjoyment in all the toil with which one toils under the sun the few days of his life which God has given him, for this is his lot (Ecclesiastes 5:18, RSV).

Do you want a verse for today that will put new style in your living? This is it, for it assures you that *it is holy for you to be happy*. It is appropriate to enjoy life. Happiness is a gift of your Creator. (The Giver likes to give, especially this One.) To be happy is your lot. (Stop that moping and move ahead with joy.) Happiness is divine. (Why apologize about it? Why try to hide it? Look happy! Live happy!) The person who is really happy has the touch of the divine within him. (He and God get together.)

Our forefathers were possessed with this same conviction and ably stated it in the Declaration of Independence.

> We hold these truths to be self-evident, that all men are created equal, that they are endowed by their Creator with certain unalienable Rights, that among these are Life, Liberty and the pursuit of HAPPINESS.

That word *unalienable* is exactly the one needed to express the fact. It means a right that can't be taken from you. You have that right forever. You were born with it.

Have you noticed how many people run after happiness? They are like the puppy who chased its own tail.

Day after day, the puppy ran in circles trying to get to its tail. One afternoon, a big dog saw the puppy chasing its tail, and the large dog said, "Why are you chasing your tail?"

"Well," replied the puppy, "I was told that happiness will be found in my tail. I want to be happy; so I have been chasing it in order to get happy. The only trouble is I never catch it."

The wiser dog said, "Do you know that I was told the same thing? But one day I didn't chase my tail, and I found out that happiness was following me wherever I went."

Filed in my memory is one of the most heartbreaking stories I've ever heard. It is about a man who wanted to be happy, but didn't have direction. "I thought a lot of money could make me happy," he recounted. "To make lots of money, I went to college and got a degree; then I got out in the business world, and I've stamped my mark on it in a moderate way. I have more money than I can spend. My wife and children want for nothing. We live in the snobbiest house on Snob-Hill. We drive the plushiest cars. And I'm miserable." His heart ached, and so did mine as I listened to him. Now, though, he has everything *plus* happiness. He cashed in on his birthright.

I like people to know that Jesus was a happy person. Life wasn't a bunch of sour grapes for Him. Someone overheard Jesus talking about Himself and wrote down these words. "Then the Son of Man came, enjoying life . . ." (Matthew 11:19, PHILLIPS). As a matter of fact, Jesus leveled some of His strongest words at frown-faced, sad-spirited people. Some in that crowd were hollow-hearted religionists. They never really responded to the positive power of religion.

I have used the term principles of happiness. There is one definite principle governing happiness: *happiness comes when you are in diligent pursuit of your best self.* Let me explain the use of *best self*. It is what you are now becoming for good. It is the actual and the in process; it is the fact in motion. Happiness depends on it. When are you in pursuit of your very best self?

You are in pursuit of your best self when you're *enjoying what you have.* There is the case of Dina Donohue, bedridden in a New York hospital.

One evening, a victim of a stroke was wheeled into her room and put into the second bed. Soon, it was dinner time and the trays were placed on the tables and rolled up to the two women. The new arrival fumbled around a bit, then burst into tears.

"It's no use. I'm good for nothing," she cried. "I can't even put sugar in my tea."

"You need two hands to do this," she insisted as she held up a paper envelope of sugar.

31

Mrs. Donohue looked over the situation, breathed a silent prayer, and said to her new companion, "Watch me."

Slipping a corner of the sugar envelope into her mouth, she tore off the opposite side with one hand. "See, you really need only one hand."

With her hand trembling, the other lady put an envelope in her mouth and tore it open. "I didn't think I could do it," she kept saying.

"Oh, I guess there are many things I can do if I figure out how."

In thinking about it, Mrs. Donohue wrote that no matter how bad off we are, we can help ourselves if we forget what we've lost and use what power we have.

Accent the positive. Minimize the negative. Putting the emphasis on your assets builds happiness from the inside out, and enables you to shape the world around you. That's what you do when you are happy over what you do have. There's no happiness in trying to live on what you don't have—plenty of agony, but no substantial happiness.

Another act in pursuing your best self is to *learn to laugh at yourself*. This kind of humor expresses your importance as a child of God who is able to rise above anything that happens to you. It helps you to see the good side of your life when you are tempted to give in to the pressures of living, yet, many people laugh only at others—never at themselves. They develop the spirit of ridicule. But every truly happy person laughs at himself occasionally, since there are conditions which come up in everyone's life that can best be handled only after seeing the humor in them.

One of the most provocative articles I've read recently is the one by Arthur Gordon entitled, "The Engaging Art of Laughing at Yourself." He describes laughing at yourself in terms of seeing yourself as others see you and smiling at what you see. Long has the personality-building power of laughter been acclaimed by knowledgeable doctors.

The prominent psychiatrist, Dr. Smiley Blanton, once made it clear that mental health is affected by self-aimed humor. He found that the turning point came for many patients when they were able to see a flicker of humor in some aspect of their situation in life. The famous doctor had seldom been called on to help a person who had a sense of the ridiculous: he never had to treat anyone who could really laugh at himself. Have you learned to laugh at yourself?

The principle of happiness includes the mountain-view concept. Apply it to situations bringing unhappiness and you will be in pursuit of your best self. Whatever the circumstance, rise up and look beyond it to the whole of life and you will see that the situation is both temporary and manageable, depending on your faith and persistence in doing something about it.

I got a lasting impression of this truth while driving in the California Sierras. That high country is lush with beauty in summertime. In a quiet place there with the sights and sounds of nature, you can feel the gentle hand of God tapping on your heart. On our trip, we came to a huge burnt-out area. The fire had swept away hundreds of acres of beauty. I turned to my wife and said, "Isn't that tragic?" I could visualize its distortion of the whole region. When we got several miles higher, we stopped to take another look at the view. Where was the scarred area? I tried to find it, but from the higher vantage point, it was swallowed up in the whole.

A party of four men climbing a mountain to enjoy the scenery had a similar experience. The first man wore new and expensive shoes which didn't fit. He complained constantly. "Oh, my feet are killing me. I don't think I can go a step farther."

The second man was obsessed with greed. As he climbed the mountain, he kept saying, "I wish that farm over there were mine. Look at that house. Why can't I have a place like that? I'm sure the owner is no better than I am."

The third climber kept his eye on the clouds overhead. "Don't those clouds look bad? Bet it's going to rain. Our day is going to be ruined. I just know it." Worry and fear squelched any happiness the climb might have brought him.

But the fourth man was really a climber. "Look at this view. Isn't it great! I feel like a new man. The climb has let loose some muscles long in a state of limbo." This man looked away from the trivial distractions and focused his attention on the whole scene. He was the happy climber.

You will never maintain happiness without applying the mountain-view concept to the situations bringing unhappiness. Without it, circumstances become uncontrollable; life gets unmanageable. You are swept away in a sea of defeatism, depression, discouragement, and a dismal outlook dims your thinking. Without this dynamic concept put to work in your life, you will find what it means to be too close to the forest to see the trees. When this happens, the sense of objectivity loses its power. In my life as a Christian minister, many people have come to me seeking help and advice. From my experience I can say that of all the problems people have encountered, this is among the biggest—failure to employ the mountain-view concept.

A salesman, who was glum and looked as if he were a wash-out from life, really felt that he was a wash-out from his job, although he had already proven himself as a top salesman. His biggest hurdle was to take on the mountain-view concept.

"Your problem, like most others, is both temporary and manageable," I reminded him. "Therefore, you can be sure that if you lend yourself to the solution, you'll work out of it."

Someone asked a man about his favorite Bible verse. After thinking a moment, he answered, "And it came to pass." That sounded strange. "And it came to pass." "But," retorted the inquirer, "that isn't a Bible verse. It's only the beginning of one." "It may not be a verse to you," replied the man, "but those are the stoutest words in all the Bible to me." He explained by saying, "It didn't come to stay—it came to *pass*." He was wise to a rule for happy living—the mountain-view concept.

You are in pursuit of your best self with *God as the prominent power in your life*. In the *Varieties of Religious Experience*, William James wrote: "We and God must have business one with the other, and in opening our hearts to him our highest destiny is fulfilled." That is the highway to happiness which another very wise man discussed by saying: ". . . Happy is he who trusts in [leans on, depends on, believes in] the Lord" (Proverbs 16:20, RSV).

How many people in chasing after happiness have set aside their Creator? Or at least reduced Him to a side-line figure? No wonder they're on an endless, empty road to futility.

Dr. Charles Allen, a good friend of mine who is one of the greatest ministers and authors in America, claims that no person becomes his best self by himself. God makes it possible for a person to develop his best self. Faith and its incomparable products nourish the best self. To me, it works in this way. Divine adequacies fill in for the inadequacies of being a human so that my life is more and more a God-filled, God-adjusted life; consequently, I become happier and happier.

HOW TO BE HAPPY

1. You can be happy. (There is every reason for you to be happy. There is not a single reason of sufficient importance to keep you from being happy.)
2. Happiness depends more on what's inside you than what is outside.
3. You can shape your surroundings. (You and God can do it.)
4. Thank God for what you have and enjoy it.
5. Take on the spirit toward life that will help you to laugh at yourself.
6. Apply the mountain-view concept to those situations which bring unhappiness.
7. Consider God the most prominent Power in your life.
8. Identify yourself with a church doing God's work, and involve yourself in a particular service through that church.

5.

—When I'm Criticized?

I've made an amazing discovery. Although it may be nothing new to you, I want to share this discovery with you! At last I have found a way to avoid criticism. Do you want to know the formula to steer clear of criticism?

Believe nothing!
Do nothing!
Dream nothing!
Expect nothing!
Plan nothing!
Say nothing!
Support nothing!
Think nothing!

During a speaking engagement in a small town, I had the opportunity to tell about the work of the Association For Inspirational Living. The Association is a nonprofit organization—not related to nor sponsored by any one church or denomination. Its purpose is to promote practical Christian principles for daily living among all people, and this is being achieved through television worship, printed sermons and booklets, and the widespread distribution of other inspirational and devotional materials.

The pastor of the church where I spoke asked about criticism. "Out of the hundreds of letters coming to your office each week, how many of them are critical?"

"About one percent-two percent," I answered.

"How does this criticism affect you?"

I said that we accept the criticisms and move ahead. Anyone who is in the game must be big enough to take the boo's as well as the cheers. As former President Harry Truman often advised his staff, "Don't go in the kitchen if you can't stand the heat."

If you want to think tall, believe big, plan powerfully, dream dynamically and roll up your sleeves and be somebody with your life, then prepare yourself for criticism.

Basically, there are two kinds of people: the Carpenters and the Criticizers. The Carpenter is a builder. He is part of the construction crew. He creates. He changes things! He makes beauty! The world needs him! God blesses him! And he is a credit to the human race!

But a Criticizer is a mental cannibal who feasts on the short-comings of others. The Criticizer is a captive imprisoned by his own faults. The Criticizer is a casualty of his own inadequacies. And the Criticizer makes for himself a cesspool of filth in which he has to wade. It would not be such a bad idea for the Criticizer to hide himself permanently, for these times demand Carpenters, not Criticizers. A man who had only one talent was asked, "And what is that one talent?"

"The talent of criticism," he replied.

"Well," suggested the questioner, "maybe you'd better do the same thing with *your* talent that the man of one talent in the parable did—go and bury it. Anybody whose only ability is to criticize might as well bury it, and himself with it."

Criticism means to make a critical estimate of someone or something; to pass judgment with respect to merits or defects; to point out faults; to judge adversely; to express disapproval; and to censure.

Even Jesus Christ, the Master Carpenter by trade and spirit, wasn't a stranger to criticism! (That should offer some consolation.) Who among all men is better qualified than He to advise,

Be happy when people criticize you and perpetrate evil words against you and speak all kinds of slanderous and untrue stories

37

about you. Be glad! Be full of joy, for you will be abundantly cared for by your God! (Matthew 5:11-12 paraphrased).

When you are criticized, do you run away or do you face up to it with determination to outlive it? Do you sink into a tight little shell or do you double your efforts to do good? Do you give up or do you give more? Do you give out or do you give in?

A young college professor, who is a personal friend of mine, was severely criticized for something which he had nothing to do with. Later, he was exonerated, but at first Harold wanted to lash out, fire for fire, at the perpetrators of it all. "Then I wanted to quit and get myself a job at another school," he said. Finally, his decision was to outlive the criticism by staying there through it, and by doing all the good he could. He commented, "I've not been sorry for staying—not for a moment."

You can outlive any criticism, but there are laws for creative Christian treatment of criticism just as there are laws for good golfing. I do not profess to be a pro on the course, but I do play the game occasionally. While playing a few rounds recently, I was reminded of my obvious need to give more attention to those laws of golf.

My first wood shot ended up in the rough. You know that there is a fairway and a rough on every hole, but from the place I play, you'd think there is no fairway at all. On the very next hole, I landed in the rough again, and it was about the same shot to the green as the previous hole. "Oh," I thought, "I'll use the same club as before. And if I keep my eye on the ball, maintain a straight left arm, conduct a smooth, rhythmic swing and follow through, I'll have a good shot. Those are basic laws of the game; observe them, Ray, for once in your life."

I walked up to the ball, took a practice swing, looked to see if the two Presbyterian elders I had as partners were watching, got set, made the customary gyrations with the back portion of the body and swung. I don't know which went farthest—the ball, the club, or the clod of dirt. (All three combined might have totaled fifty feet. I hope the elders weren't watching!)

The laws of golf are still intact. So are the laws for creative Christian treatment of criticism. Observe them. Get compatible with them, and you can deal with criticism so that God will be praised, immensely; you will be happy, exuberantly; and those around you will be inspired, inevitably.

If you are doing anything worthwhile in life, prepare yourself to accept criticism without letting it throw you into a state of disorganization. I remember a seminary classmate who, after fifteen months as pastor of his first church, was approached by a lay-leader and told he was a wonderful man, but that his messages, prayers and a few personal practices of his were puny. That was on Monday morning, and Friday, my phone rang and I was told about the situation.

"I haven't been able to eat, sleep, study, visit, or do much of anything all week," my friend said. "My whole life has been confused." He was in an acute state of disorganization over criticism. Since then, however (for his good and that of the church), he has learned to accept criticism without letting it choke him emotionally. Have you learned this practical lesson?

Keep your emotional control center calm. No one can function at peak efficiency when he is irate, disordered and mixed-up. This is true of parents as well as presidents.

In my neighborhood there are many children, two of whom are my own. Ample opportunity is afforded there to keep control. For example, I watched an angered man repeatedly ring the door-bell at a neighbor's house. When the neighbor answered, he was greeted by an aroused father who bellowed, "Your son. . . . He ran over my cactus with his stupid bicycle. My prize cactus! I've told him a thousand times not to get close to my cacti. I demand that you do something about that little. . . ."

"Thank you for telling me," the neighbor replied. "I'll check into it and I'll be happy to replace your prize cactus. We'll work this out."

Now, I thought, that is the way to do it. He was organized and in charge of himself when confronted with anger.

"Oh, well. O.K.," quipped the cactus lover meekly. His silly attitude had been shown up and he knew it. He tucked his hands in his pockets and apologetically slipped away.

A doctor who outlined some basic qualities necessary for achievement included frustration tolerance, self-questioning, living with competition, and *accepting criticism*. Sometimes it may be true that the bigger your life becomes, the bitterer becomes the criticism; so take criticism in the stride of life.

Something else you can do when you are criticized is to consider the criticism sensibly and prayerfully. Ask yourself: Is it true? Is it right? What can I learn from it? As an intelligent child of God, you can search out the opportunities which can be found—yes, even through a fault-finding, judgmental, censuring and, perhaps shortsighted, human being.

One of the secretaries on my office staff wrote on the back of an attendance card the comment of a new family in our church. Upon reading the comment, I asked the secretary for more information about it, saying, "What can we learn from this?" You can turn every criticism into an opportunity to grow and mature.

Newsman William Ryan of Associated Press wrote an article shortly after Russia's invasion of Czechoslovakia in 1967 entitled, "Soviets Just Can't Take Criticism." Mr. Ryan said that the Communist system does not dare permit free expression, and that it is afraid of reform. That Communism cannot stand criticism betrays a basic weakness in the system.

There are people who can't take criticism because their systems are weak. They don't know what to do with criticism once they've got it. It can offer an opportunity, but they don't see it. Instead, they stagger around in a dizzy and dazed emotional state woeing themselves into defeat. Prayer and common sense can turn criticism into triumph for you.

At the age of twenty-six, David Nunn was the head of an automobile financing and insurance firm, because he had sensibly and prayerfully considered criticism. Others told him he couldn't do it, "After all, your dad doesn't own the agency!" Some people very close to my friend Dave Nunn had challenged him: they said he was too young to aspire to such a high position.

"Do I have the background?" he asked himself. "Do I have the enthusiasm and dedication it takes to be a manager? Do I have the know-how? Am I willing to learn?"

After answering yes to his questions, he began the surge up; and he got there, but only when he saw the opportunity in criticism. It fired him up for the climb.

When you're criticized, it is profitable to consider the source of the criticism. Doctors point out the wisdom of this when they talk about the danger of criticizing others. The peril is not so much that someone else is verbally cut up, but that the truth is coming out about the one doing the criticizing. Jesus referred to it when he spoke to a group of people in these words,

> Don't criticize people. . . . Why do you look at the speck of sawdust in your brother's eye and fail to notice the plank in your own (Matthew 7:1-3, PHILLIPS).

Modern psychology has definitely illustrated that the mirror effect is a common trait in our personality patterns; that is, what you criticize in others could very well be a mirror reflecting your own fault. In *Psychology and Morals*, J. A. Hadfield claims it is actually true that in criticizing others a person is broadcasting his own faults. This is precisely what the old philosopher realized when he said, "It is literally true that in judging others we trumpet abroad our secret faults."

A criticizer is putting himself on trial much like the visitor in a Los Angeles art gallery who, looking over the work done by the masters, said to a procurator, "I don't care for these pictures." The man replied, "My friend, you are on trial here—not the pictures."

If someone belittles you, more often than not, he is only trying to cut you down to *his* size. Such a person burdens himself with a fault-finding frame of mind and keeps himself poor with a critical way of life.

Whatever the criticism may be, move ahead, keep going and drive on to the best of your ability. God made you for this purpose. It is an everyday-life example of man over matter and materialism. You are created to conquer! The Bible tells about it in the Old Testament book of Psalms.

When I look at thy heavens, the work of thy fingers,
the moon and the stars which thou hast established;
what is man that thou art mindful of him,
and the son of man that thou dost care for him?
Yet thou hast made him little less than God,
and dost crown him with glory and honor.
Thou hast given him dominion over the works of thy hands;
thou hast put all things under his feet,
all sheep and oxen, and also the beasts of the field,
the birds of the air, and the fish of the sea,
whatever passes along the paths of the sea.

O Lord, our Lord,
how majestic is thy name in all the earth (Psalms 8:3-9, RSV)!

Men are demonstrating this passage more and more. While dealing with the many problems of geography and climate in the building of the Panama Canal, Colonel George Goethals had to live with carping criticism from countless busybodies back home. His critics contemptuously predicted that the great task would never be completed, but the resolute builder pressed steadily forward in his work and said nothing.

A criticism-conscious assistant asked, "Aren't you going to answer your critics?"

"In time," replied Goethals.

"How?" queried the subordinate.

The great engineer smiled and answered, "With the canal!"

Move ahead. Keep going. Drive on!

WHAT TO DO WHEN YOU'RE CRITICIZED

1. Attempt the biggest things you can.
2. Challenge yourself with great dreams.
3. Make sure you are a carpenter instead of a criticizer.
4. Stay in charge of yourself, no matter what the criticism is nor how vehement it becomes.
5. Apply everyday sense and prayer to criticism.
6. Accept the opportunity to grow and mature offered by criticism.
7. Claim your God-granted superiority.
8. Move ahead with enthusiasm and determination.

6.

—When I Have Those Sleepless Nights?

Shakespeare once wrote that gentle sleep is nature's soft nurse. For some people, time which should be given to sleeping is a drawn out fit of fury. They're restless; they toss and turn; they're nervous and jittery. At the break of dawn, when it's time to get up to a bright and wonderful new day, they're pooped out and drooped out. Their faces often are etched with the lines of miserable tiredness, and their eyes are as heavy as lead. But for many other people—those who really sleep—it is a healing, restful, relaxing, refreshing and re-creative experience. My father-in-law, H. C. Eubanks, is a man who knows this for himself, and he can sleep through almost anything.

Years ago, he slept through the yelling of neighborhood children as they stomped, clattered and chattered in the house enroute to the favorite ice cream box on the block (which happened to be in his kitchen). It gets very noisy when somebody is taking piano lessons, yet he added a deep, rhythmic, melodious snore of his own to the tunes stroked out by an enterprising daughter. (And he slept not more than a few feet away from the piano, too!) Night or day—summer, fall, spring, or winter—there was no difference in his sleeping capabilities, and nothing worries him. In his advanced years, his hair is all there and it is jet black—not a gray blade in sight anywhere.

One day I asked, "Doc, how do you do it? What's your secret for sleeping so soundly?"

"Why, David," he replied in his deep drawl, "I go there to sleep." Just as simple and definite as that. I expected some protracted explanation, touching on the philosophical side of soothing slumber; but he put it all in five magnificent words, "I go there to sleep."

Consider this in regard to church. Apparently, some people do go *there* to sleep, or at least they find slumber is irresistibly induced while they're at church. (Considering what some ministers are saying these days, maybe it is just as well for the congregation to take a few naps in the pew!) It occurred to me that some worshippers in my own congregation think the different sound levels in my voice are deliberately used as devices to keep people awake during the sermon, but that theory was mercilessly decimated by an experience I had while on vacation one year.

We were driving back to our destination after attending another church. Jerry, our eleven-year-old son, said he liked our church more than the one we had just visited. I agreed with him, but, not suspecting any shady reasoning, I asked why he liked our church more than the other one. "Because," said Jerry confidently, "I can sleep better in ours." A worshipper in my church once told me that he started coming to the church on the advice of his physician. "How's that?" I queried, again without suspecting what I was about to hear.

"Well," retorted the man, "I went to the doctor about my insomnia. Oh, it was awful, and he told me to take these pills and go to church." (I am not sure the man understood the meaning of his doctor's advice, for ever since then he has methodically dozed in the pew!)

Suppose you were to go to sleep during a violent storm, when your very life was greatly endangered and when the full use of your senses might save your life? That would be a classic display of foolishness, wouldn't it? It most certainly would be an insult to religious faith, for faith exercises the intellect, and you wouldn't be using your thinking cap if you slept under such conditions.

45

But suppose you were to go to sleep when ideal weather conditions existed, and then a mighty storm blew up? This is what Jesus did many centuries ago, and the storm didn't bother Him, apparently. He must have been a tight sleeper—no doubt a snorer. The Man of Galilee exercised a long-used spiritual exercise for sound sleeping on tough nights. Additionally, the prescription for sleep which worked so amazingly with Him is still the best inducer of slumber that any human being can find. It is *faith*—a pure, performing, practical religious faith. I have seen such faith work wonders with multitudes of modern men, and I've witnessed its power to overcome the roughest problems a person can meet.

Consider, for example, a good friend of mine, Harold Johnson. As one of the top-rated engineers on the West Coast, Harold has an illustrious career spanning two decades. Still a young man in every respect, he is planning and plodding with the spirit of a teen-ager. As president of a civil engineering firm which bears his name, Harold has his finger on the business pulse of America, particularly Southern California.

"Business has had its ups and downs, " Harold volunteered in conversation. He was making reference to the drop-off in housing construction which Southern California experienced at one time. That is his bread and butter, but the stiff business challenge was met with a dogged religious faith that wouldn't quit or fall in to despair.

"Yes," he commented, "back then, Tish [his lovely wife] and I had to reorganize. In the process, I had to let faithful employees go. It hurt me to release those good people, but they understood. Say, do you see that Book over there?" He was pointing to a Bible on the utility desk near the conference table in his large office. "Believe me, that has become an unrelenting resource of strength for me. And the other materials—see them? They helped to pull me through, and they've become a steady stream of spiritual and mental vitamins to me—a part of my daily diet," he said with a grin. Harold was speaking of the fine assortment of inspirational writings by Norman Vincent Peale, Charles L. Allen and others.

Faith, religious faith, has a big and growing hand in Harold's up-styled life; yet some moderns still have the futile notion that faith is the fairy-tale answer to namby-pamby living for nilly-willy people. Leading thinkers of our star-studded age know better.

Isn't it important to have some idea as to what this faith is? It is an act of self-dedication in which the will, mind (intellect) and emotions (affection) have their places. Furthermore, faith is the determination to live as if certain things are true; then, it will be discovered that they are true. By living as if they are real, they will become real. In the process, we change, and we find that things change to fit our views. Perhaps the definition from William James, quoting William Salter, gives more insight to this faith: "The essence of courage is to stake one's life on a possibility; the essence of faith is to believe that the possibility exists."

Both explanations of faith are up-to-date variations of the one made in the New Testament by a man of faith. "To have faith is to be sure of the things we hope for, to be certain of the things we cannot see" (Hebrews 11:1, TEV).

When His boat-buddies cried out for their lives, Jesus countered enthusiastically with this searching statement, "O men of little faith" (Matthew 8:26, RSV). The question here is simply: How does this faith work best for sleeping peacefully? Now we get involved with some realistic spiritual techniques to take good care of those sleepless nights.

I am indebted to thoughtful people who give me illustrations, quotes and the like which can be used in my sermons and writings. One Sunday during worship, a member meditated on an up-coming message. He scribbled his ideas down on the back of an offering envelope, which he handed to me after the service. This is what I read: "Where Are You, God—When I Have Those Sleepless Nights? or Pastor's Prescription For A Peaceful P.M., or Rev. Ray's Rules For Rewarding, Radiant Rest, or How To Become A Sleeping Pill." We are interested in Faith's Facts For Dandy Dozing, in the jargon of my friend. The point is, faith can put sound sleep into your night.

In the first place, *faith*, if practiced, *prevails on the will to let you go to sleep*. The will is a big part of one's being, as illustrated

47

by the man who told me that he had looked over a certain car he was thinking about buying. For two months, he had it in his heart to purchase an automobile, and I knew it; so I said, "When you get down to it, you've already bought the car."

He looked at me as if I were rather strange and replied, "Oh, yeah! What makes you say that?"

I answered, "You bought it in your will two months ago. Mentally, you signed the sales contract then. Now, all that's left is to translate the will into reality. In other words, about all that is left for you to do is to put down the money and pick up the car." And the next day he did.

The same application can be made to sleeping. Will to do it strongly enough and you will sleep, through faith; for faith alone offers the energy enormous enough to rightfully prevail on the will to pursue a certain course of action, regardless of the odds and obstacles.

"Doc" Eubanks said that his secret for sound sleeping, if indeed he has such a secret, is, "I go there to sleep," or, "My objective is sleep and sleep I shall." The will to sleep is strong in him. It prevails over the foes of sleep. It overpowers the viruses of insomnia, and for more than sixty-five years he has been a healthy sleeper.

A most perceptive man of modern times gives us some insight on the will in these words: "First make sure that what you aspire to accomplish is worth accomplishing." Sleep is worthwhile. God has a design for your system. ". . . he [The Lord] gives to his beloved sleep" (Psalms 127:2 RSV). Then throw your whole vitality into what you wish to accomplish. Will it! What's worth doing is worth doing well! (Sleep included.)

Faith lived and thought puts sound sleep in your night in that faith guides the will and faith goads the will. When I feel the old nervous bug, that nagging parasite to restful sleep, starting its job, I like to ask, "Where is your faith, David Ray?"

To anchor the will, you need commitment to God. Make it *total commitment*. There are the in-and-outers of commitment who have an up-and-down life, and the all-outers. These are the 100-percenters, the move-aheaders. *Faith, if practiced, powers you on to commitment to the Lord, and this commitment makes it possible for you to sleep.*

48

John Klein, a young friend in my life, is an all-American collegiate wrestler, stoutly and trimly built, and a devoutly committed man—an enthusiast for God. John directs the wrestling team for an interchurch organization which is doing a marvelous job in presenting the positive Christian message of faith and values to collegians. (We ought to hear more about this side of the young men and women in our universities. We're consistently fed the sorry happenings of campus chaos when there is so much more good going on, and I believe the good is more worthy of our attention than the bad.)

The wrestling team, under John's guidance, follows a busy schedule of matches with leading universities all over the country. During half time, these sparkling and creative young Christian men share their thrilling faith with the audience, which consists mostly of college students.

To provide his meager salary, John depends on interested people. When I heard the amount of it, I wondered how he ate. Furthermore, some of those who make commitments don't come through with payment. "But," John said with a radiance on his face as we talked about it, "God always provides when He is guiding us. . . . What God calls me to do, God makes possible in every way for me to do."

"Commitment. John," I said, "you know the ecstasy of commitment to God. And that takes faith."

This relates to sleep for the housewife, the business man, the student, the corporation executive, the senior citizen—anybody. A while ago, an extensive study was made of the sleeping habits of modern Americans, then *McCall's Magazine* reported the findings. Concisely stated, they are:

Anxieties about sleep are self-defeating. Physiologically, our emotions directly interfere with sleep—for example, by increasing blood pressure and muscular tension and by bringing into play the stimulating chemicals released through the action of the nervous system. These physical changes further trigger anxieties, and we are caught, wide-awake, in a vicious circle.

49

Perhaps our parents knew better than we how to approach the unknown land of sleep. (The old generation isn't so dumb after all, is it?) In their periods of quiet reading before bedtime, they introduced a smooth interlude between the whirl of the day's activities and the withdrawal to sleep. And in their bedtime prayers, they made explicit their resignation to rest and their submission to unconsciousness. "In your hands I entrust my spirit," says the Orthodox Jew before sleep; and throughout the world, religious people have devoted the last minutes of the day to prayer and meditation. With the burdens of the day shouldered to the best of their abilities, presidents, statesmen and kings have placed their souls in trust, and accepted sleep.

Before you finally retire in the evening, commit every concern to God. Say, "Lord, here's this matter. I turn it over to You for tonight. And, God, here's so-and-so. We've had a difficult time with each other today, but I'm committing so-and-so to You for the night." Stamp the word *committed* across your mind. Think of it many times. Press it hard there. This is to make use of the power of repetition. Hardly ever in life are all systems go at the same time, and hardly ever in sleep will you find that there is a complete absence of things which will cause insomnia if a person allows them to. Then it is necessary to apply the faith-power which comes through repetition.

Repeat a certain thing often enough and it becomes a habit. Repeat the habit often enough and it becomes ingrained in your subconscious self. At that time, habit becomes automatic reflex, but it stays a habit by continual use and exercise.

By imprinting the word *committed* on your mind for each concern, and for every person who gets to you, the power of repetition goes to work for you. Then if the concern, or so-and-so, reappears during the evening, you can assuredly affirm, "I've already committed this to God. It's in good hands for the night." Insist on that affirmation, and sleeplessness will edge away.

This practical treatment of faith was impressed on me when, as a young man just starting in the Christian faith, I was told by Dr. Ben Pearson, "David, when the tempter comes around, you tell him that your life is committed to God, and he will have to take his business up with the Lord." I have never forgotten that good advise from a Christlike man, and it has spared me many sleepless nights.

Another thing faith does to help you sleep is this: *faith,* if practiced, *persuades you to do the very best you can with each day.* Faith produces. Faith perspires.

Such was the case with the boy who asked the farmer for a job. "Will you work?" the farmer asked.

"Yes, sir," answered the boy. "I can sleep soundly on a windy night." The farmer had no idea what the fellow meant by that answer.

"H-m-m-m," the farmer meditated. "And can I depend on you to take care of the barn, cows and chickens?"

"Absolutely," blurted out the boy. "I tell you I can sleep soundly on a windy night." There was that phrase again. Although the farmer had grave doubts as to the boy's mental stability, he gave him the job.

The farmer found the boy to be a great worker. Every day he gave all he had. Then one night, a storm rocked the farm. "Wake up and help me tie down the hay and secure the barn," the farmer yelled at the boy, but it was to no avail. The lad was sound asleep, so the farmer rushed out to do it himself. But when he got to the haystack, he found it well tied down, and the barn was already secure, and the animals were in shelter. Then he realized what the boy meant by, "I can sleep soundly on a windy night." Having done the best he could do, he left the rest with God.

What a technique for sleep! And faith persuades you to do your best. Having honestly done it, you can doze confidently. Anyone who hasn't done his best can find relief by sincerely accepting God's forgiveness, by making whatever amends he can, by resolving to change and start doing the best he can and by going out and doing it.

Another thing about faith is that it can *prevent nervousness from getting the best of you.* A physician told me that much of today's insomnia comes about through nervousness. It is a jittery sensation in the stomach and it has a whirlwind effect in the mind. "Millions of Americans," he claimed (on valid grounds), "lie awake at night in a suspension of nerves."

Within twenty-four hours after the doctor and I discussed it, a man came by to see me about this problem. "How can I help you?" I asked.

"I'm a nervous wreck," he replied reluctantly. "It's choking my life away." It didn't take long to recognize that he needed a doctor's assistance, and probably some counseling, but I felt that a minister might provide the added ingredient necessary for a full recovery.

Oh, was he jittery! He was restless in the chair. There seemed to be a gnawing dissatisfaction inside him. His eyes fluttered unnaturally. His speech was slightly hampered by stuttering. He jammed his words together to the extent that sometimes they were almost unintelligible. An overly nervous person usually acquires quirks like these symptomatic of his condition, including inordinate body reactions, contortions of the face and unrelaxed use of hands and arms. He had them all, it seemed, and was fidgety, uneasy, tense and fearful. No wonder he appeared rather beaten! I commented, "You need some sleep, don't you?"

"Do I!" he exclaimed. "I haven't had a good night's snooze this year."

Along with professional help, he needed the power of faith. And he needed to practice faith—live it—in that way which keeps nervousness at bay. Over a period of time, his nervousness changed to confidence and the quirks disappeared. Faith came alive in its powerful glory, and regular sleep became a stable part of his life. As a matter of fact, his return to sound sleeping was among the first visible indications of progress.

Do you know what causes you to become a nerve-punctured human being? Hurried living is one vandal. Hurry, hurry, hurry— a call of modern life that needs to fall on deaf ears.

Faith says, "You'll make it better without that rushed feeling. Your God has made you to live life on smooth strokes instead of jerky, hurried days." Faith keeps you constructively busy; at the same time it keeps you from hurrying yourself into flavorless living. At the day's end, you can thank God for a great day from which you have a sense of satisfaction within you. In place of the hurried feeling straggling into bed with you, there is a quiet, peaceful warmth to lead you into beautiful sleep.

Something else regarding faith and its aid to life-building sleep is that *faith persists in eliminating worry from your night.* (Remember that worry is a division of the mind which breaks down the processes for full and joyful living.) An American philosopher of wide reputation stated that the sovereign cure for worry is religious faith, and it gives a new zest for life, more life, a larger, richer, and more productive life.

For a worry-troubled man, I outlined a formula of faith which handles worry. After using it for several months, he told me that it was very helpful to him. Use this formula, keeping in mind that worry is the mind's reaction to a problem, real or imaginary; and that problem may be yourself, someone else, or a condition of life —either temporary or permanent.

F Face the problem directly. (It has been said that a winner is different from a loser in that the winner goes through a problem, whereas a loser goes around it, but never gets past it.)

A Admit your trust in God who is your Friend and Companion. (He will guide you to keep the worry out of your problem.)

I Instill in your mind that you have every reason to work out your problem and no reason is sufficient enough to cause you worry.

T Tend to your problem, believing that it will give way to faith-powered attention.

H Honor your Creator by maintaining, without flinching, that He made you to live without worry.

Dr. Carl Jung in his book, *Modern Man In Search Of A Soul* elaborates on religious faith.

Among all my patients in the second half of life—that is to say, over thirty-five—there has not been one whose problem in the last resort was not that of finding a religious outlook on life. It is safe to say that every one of them fell ill because he had lost that which the living religions of every age have given to their followers, and none of them has been really healed who did not regain his religious outlook.

By putting honest-to-goodness faith where the worry is, you will find sleep to be, as Sheakspeare said, "nature's soft nurse."

SPIRITUAL TECHNIQUES TO SLEEP TIGHT EVERY NIGHT

1. Faith is the greatest power for sleeping known to man.
2. This faith has to be lived. (It's a performing, practical faith.)
3. Will to sleep with all your heart and you will sleep.
4. Put Commitment to God in your night.
5. Utilize the Power of Repetition by impressing "Committed" across your thoughts time and time again.
6. Give life the best you've got. (It brings on sound sleeping—emotionally and physically.)
7. Keep busy at life, but do away with hurried living.
8. Let faith help you keep worry out of your life.

7.

—When I've Lost Control
of My Emotions?

When the young girl and her mother walked into my office for that evening appointment, both of them were in deep emotional shock. They had found out the day before that the daughter was pregnant.

"Only fifteen years old," cried the mother, "going on sixteen. She has never been this kind of girl. What happened? What happened?" The mother broke out in heavy perspiration even though the office was comfortably air conditioned.

Said the girl, "I know that I've done wrong and this is the result of it." She had the courage and integrity to admit her mistake, unlike a breed of insensible thinkers in our nation who want us to believe that we have evolved to a moral ethic that makes immorality acceptable! "The permissive society" is what a bearded rebel against life told me it should be. "My life is ruined," she sobbed.

But it wasn't ruined. Certainly there was an interruption—but not ruined.

I have always approached such situations not on a *was* basis (a shame-on-you basis), but on an *is* basis. ("This is the way it is now—now let's do something about it.") Take the matter from where it is and make the very best out of it. The person in such a situation is not deserving of a scathing, pious rebuke. (No human being is degraded enough to get that, no matter what he has done.) Before talking about the future and making some plans to handle the child, I picked up a Bible from my desk. As I

55

flipped it open to the Psalms, I said, "Let's get the present moment under control. This will help us put feelings in check."

> Bless [praise] the Lord, o my soul,
>   and forget not all his benefits,
> who forgives all your iniquity [sins],
>   who heals your diseases . . .
>
> He does not deal with us according to
>   our sins,
> nor requite [repay] us according to
>   our iniquities [sins].
>
> For as the heavens are high above the earth,
>   so great is his steadfast love toward
>   those who fear [reverence] him;
> As far as the east is from the west,
>   so far does he remove our transgressions
>   from us.
>
> As a father [a good one] pities [sympathizes
>   with] his children,
> so the Lord pities those who fear
>   [reverence] him.
>
>> (Psalms 103:2, 10-13, RSV).

As I read this, I looked at the girl occasionally. From her appearance, the Bible was really working for her. She was experiencing relief. The anxieties were being flushed out of her, and Mother, too. The despairing looks slowly changed to those of working faith. "With the Lord's help, we can work this out to a satisfactory conclusion," I assured them. I asked if the two of them wanted to join me in a prayer. Both did.

That wasn't the end of the matter, and not all of the problem was solved by Bible reading and prayer. But what a healthy beginning! What motivation and strength they provided! A placid calmness came to them. Without this control, nothing could have been accomplished.

America's aquanauts have found out about the stresses of pressure on the ocean's floor. America's astronauts have found out about the stresses of an environment thousands of miles into God's great universe. But, according to doctors, the most important stress of all is that of the stressing emotions.

Dr. John Schlindler wrote in his book, *How To Live 365 Days A Year*, that emotional stress can be greater than any other stress. Emotions usually act for a longer time than do other stressors, and they can produce the same effects as any other type of stress.

I define *emotion* as a state of mind reflected in the body by a reaction, either good or bad, depending on the state of mind. There are many influences on our emotions.

The unusual power of emotions is being brought to our attention more frequently. Already we have discovered that *emotions can cause illness through the nervous system.* Physicians acknowledge that muscles can be made tight by emotions. When this happens, people have all sorts of pains, including common headaches and migraine headaches. Pains similar to those of an ulcer or gall bladder attack often occur from emotional stress.

It has also been proven that *your emotions affect your breathing.* When you are fired up, they increase your rate of breathing, which in turn can cause hyperventilation. The carbon dioxide level in your body drops until abnormal things start happening.

As a matter of fact, *your health is directly affected by your emotions.* Dr. Paul White, the famous heart specialist, illustrated this in the story of a surgeon who performed a lengthy operation on a man named Henry to remove cancer. A few days after the surgery, the doctor said that the patient was going to die. Medically, he was safe in making the prognostication, but he failed to take into account Henry's will to live and his driving optimism.

"Henry," another doctor asked as he entered the hospital room, "how are you today?"

Henry was conscious, but not much more. He managed a wan smile and replied, "Okay, Doc. And I'm going to be out of here in a few days."

Henry's attitude remained cheerful and determined, and he got well. "So what?" someone says, "He would have anyway." The

57

team of physicians attending Henry agreed that if he had accepted the emotions of despair and defeat that his condition warranted, Henry would have died.

The scientific explanation for Henry is: Good emotions, like faith and cheer, produced a maximum hormone balance in his body, making up for what medicine alone could not do. The spiritual conclusion is: Those good emotions in Henry were God's healing power and love at work on his mind and body, for what the mind genuinely and intensely desires, the body will cooperate in bringing about.

What are the two major causes of uncontrolled emotions? *Fear* is the root cause. There is a legend about a man on his way to Istanbul. He was stopped by a woman who asked for a ride. As they drove down the road, the man looked at her and became frightened.

"Who are you?" he asked.

She replied, "I'm Diphtheria."

Immediately the peasant stopped and ordered the old woman to get off and walk, but she persuaded him to take her along, on the promise that she would not kill more than five people in all of Istanbul. As a pledge of her good word, the old woman handed him a dagger which she said was the only weapon that would cause her death, saying, "I shall meet you in two days. If I break my promise, you may stab me."

In Istanbul, one hundred twenty people died during those two days. The man who had driven her to the city was furious. After finding the old woman on the street, he raised the dagger and was about to plunge it into her heart. She stopped him with the words, "I have kept my agreement. I killed only five. Fear killed the others."

People get bad emotions when they are afraid of circumstances. I witnessed this at work when Kitty met the water hose. Kitty is the cat in our family. Despite the inauspicious way he came to our house (brought by some church members without my knowledge), Kitty has carved his way into our affections. It was

58

love at first sight between our son, Jerry, and daughter, Darla, and Kitty.

As I watered some flowers one evening, Kitty slipped out of the garage to look the situation over. He had never seen a water hose before, nor had he heard the sound of water as it sprays out of the hose. These were unknown circumstances to Kitty. Several times he ran back into the safety of the garage. But as he became acquainted with the water hose and its noise, he realized that it was not there to harm him. Neither are the circumstances in your life there to hurt you; rather, they can help you. Fear no circumstance!

People also get foul emotions when they are afraid of confrontations with other people. Imagination usually is hard at work in this fear point. The power of your imagination is utterly fantastic, but it is the negative use of imagination which works on those no-good emotions, especially in this area of people-to-people confrontation. You *think* a confrontation. Ninety percent of them never come off.

I remember a woman who had broken out in a horrible red rash because of imagined confrontations. "There's nothing wrong with you," her doctor said after he examined her thoroughly. She went to him expecting to get news of some serious malady. After all, she had never broken out in a red rash before in her life!

Something *was* wrong, and the physician had keen enough insight to recognize it. "Your rash is being caused by something other than an organic disorder," he calmly suggested. "What crucial situation have you faced recently?"

It didn't take the woman more than a moment to say, "My husband and his job. He is thinking of changing jobs. Now, doctor, that might not seem like such an important thing, but my husband is an important man with a position that most men would give their eye-teeth to have. I'm proud of him, very proud; but now, he's almost convinced that a new opportunity is the challenge he wants. We have established friends. What will *they think* if my Bob goes into this new work? It hasn't been tried here, yet. What if he fails at it? What will happen to our standing in the community?"

That question, "What will *they think?*" causes more ridiculous heartbreak than we'll ever know. It comes out of *fear*—fear of confrontations with other people.

As for the woman with the rash, the husband made the decision to start the new business (with her reserved agreement) and, I am happy to report, he has done far better than ever before. The rash lasted for six weeks, but within ten days after the definite commitment was made to launch out in the new venture, she returned to normal. The ugly red rash had disappeared. Through the help of a very wise physician and faith, she reached a plateau where she was no longer afraid of what *they* might *think*.

Basically, it is fear of oneself—what one knows or doesn't know about himself—that projects one into uncontrolled emotions. More and more, religion and psychiatry are combining to make better, happier Christians all across this land. The two complement one another. Psychiatry is helping us to find out more about ourselves. Authentic religion helps people gain power to put that knowledge to work, to overcome those inadequacies and to live with a new, happy, triumphant style. Apply the principles of Christianity and you can spell death for fear of yourself.

This kind of fear, though, is the worst type in that it is the rawest sort of affront to the most precious gift Almighty God has given you—*yourself*. Where has that fear of yourself come from? You weren't born with it. As a small child, you had a faith in the goodness of life. You had a smile for others. Hope beamed through your eyes and you were joyous. You were quick to forgive your playmates and get over those little misunderstandings. (Wouldn't it be glorious if grown-ups were as swift to forgive and forget? Human relationships would be infinitely better than they are.)

Apparently, something has happened since birth to bring on this fear. It has been developed. Possibly, parents and environment contributed. Maybe you were inculcated with the rotten stuff. But now, you stand on your own feet. You can change and eliminate the fear-of-yourself disease! Why be afraid of you? God made you. Put an end to that fear!

Another way people lose control of their emotions is by *feeling empty*. When empty, you feel helpless; you feel alienated. This sense of nothingness generates discouragement, then depression, then despair. Often, this awful emptiness comes when you're not doing something worthy of your energies; or, you feel empty when your job doesn't measure up to a big challenge. I have seen men overcome by despair when their responsibilities didn't seem to match their inner energies.

We need tough challenges and mighty demands. I got the point of this truth from a story of Man o' War in the book, *Success Through A Positive Mental Attitude*, by W. Clement Stone and Napoleon Hill.

It was billed as the race of the century. That sunny afternoon in July, 1920, indomitable Man o' War was pitted against the challenger, John P. Grier, in the Dwyer Stakes. Man o' War had already run his way into the racing hall of fame. That afternoon, he showed how. He responded to a tough, really tough, challenge with all the inner resources a great horse can draw on.

John P. Grier was no fluke. Many enthusiasts were sure that Man o' War had reached his peak and that the outcome of this race would force him to move over and make room for John P. Grier.

At the bell, both horses leaped off to a quick start. At the first turn, they were neck and neck. They rounded the second turn so evenly that fans couldn't tell which horse had the edge. Thousands of people, acting as if one person, leaped up from their seats magnetized by the thrilling moment. Suddenly, John P. Grier surged in front; he was beginning to pull away. Was the immortal Man o' War finished?

Never had Man o' War felt the sharp sting of the jockey's whip. Never had it been necessary. The great horse seemed to have a natural instinct that caused him to make the surge forward at just the right moment. The jockey knew this. But Man o' War was not responding naturally with that surge at Aqueduct that day.

The time for action was upon him. The jockey slipped the whip down the horse's side and whisked a sharp blow to the flanks of the magnificent animal. As if spurred on from a new-found

61

reservoir of energy, Man o' War spurted ahead. The crowd's roar was like a fleet of airplanes turned up ready for take-off. Never had they seen Man o' War pound the turf with such precision and power. At the finish line, he was more than two lengths ahead of John P. Grier.

He needed the tough challenge. Men do, too. The big challenge, which forces you to dig deep into the power supply inside, will make a big person out of you.

Jesus was a person who never flinched from a situation which called for His deepest resources, you will notice as you read the Gospels.

What are you going to do to control your emotions? Fear, as a negative emotion from which uncontrolled and bad emotions come, needs to be replaced by positive emotions. There are several effective methods which you may find helpful in replacing fear.

Put your fear out in the open where you can investigate it. Many people are afraid of what they don't know. Ask them what they fear and they can't answer it definitely; yet, that fear straps them spiritually and mentally. Throw your fear out on the table. Take an honest look at it. Once you look at what you are afraid of, you probably will no longer fear it. As you probe your fears honestly and openly, keep in mind that fear thrives on exaggerations.

Remember that the main cause of fear is the condition within you rather than the conditions around you. Fear becomes the mental feedback to its own predicament. Often I advise people that if they don't have fear inside, there is nothing from the outside that can scare them. But there is a potent third force in taking care of fear. *It must be replaced with the positive emotion of trust.* There is no way to fear what you trust.

Dr. Alfred Adler, the famous psychiatrist, tells of the time he didn't trust himself; as a result, he was afraid of himself.

In college, everyone told him he couldn't cope with math. There wasn't any doubt about it, they thought. Young Adler simply could not solve the problems. Well, before long, Adler himself began thinking that way. He got to the place where he was afraid to tackle a problem. One day, the tide began to change and Adler began to trust himself. "Maybe I can work this stuff," he thought.

At a class session, the professor put a problem on the board that no one could work. The brainiest student in the class sat dumbfounded. Adler said, "I believe I can do it." As he walked up to the board, muffled chuckles and low-tone giggles could be heard throughout the room. To the amazement of the class, Adler did solve the problem. He had replaced fear with trust.

Underline it in your mind: You fear only that which you distrust. Affirm in your own mind that you don't have to be afraid of anything or anybody anywhere. Religious faith—a life-changing trust in God Almighty—is one of the well-proven replacements for fear. A friend of mine related how he overcame fear by using this spiritual rule.

It was late afternoon. The resident doctor had given me word that the surgeon would operate on me the next morning. A certain nervousness and fear came over me. I got out my daily devotional guide and my Bible to read before trying to sleep. My attention was drawn to this verse, "My presence shall go with you, and I will give you rest" (Exodus 33:14, rsv). That promise was to me as well as to Moses. Fear and nervousness fled.

There is still another way to control your emotions: *use yourself for the good of others.* This is the outlet by which you share yourself with people. Psychology and religion have recognized the problem of dammed-up anxiety. People worry when they have no interest in helping others.

There is a cherished letter in my file which came from a spritely seventy-six-year-old man who has enjoyed a full life and a great deal of success in business. He said that throughout his life, he strived to remember his father's advice to pray, to honor God in what he did, to take each day as it comes, and always to look for a chance to help the other guy. That advice is good for any age, but the point for writing the letter was to tell me that, in his leisure years, he had found the most joy in life helping people at the Braille Institute two days a week, and volunteering himself for extra responsibilities at his church.

Every person has some abilities which he can use creatively in helping people. Whether you are twenty-five or eighty-five, you need this outlet. God made you that way.

In Southern California, people like to swim a great deal. To swim, however, a person has to do more than dabble his feet around the edges of the pool. He must do more than wade around in the shallow end. He must get into the water. You can control your emotions and really live; but you have to do more than dabble at the edge. You must involve yourself.

WHAT TO DO TO CONTROL YOUR EMOTIONS

1. Think of God as your Friend.
2. Affirm that you don't need to be afraid of anything or anybody.
3. Welcome stiff challenges with the thought that they help build you into a tough person.
4. Draw on the deep spiritual and mental power in you.
5. Approach every condition with the thought, "God and I can work this out together."
6. When you're tempted to give in to wild and bad emotions, repeat this: The quieting, healing hand of God is upon me now. He takes away this bad emotion. In its place, I have faith to be composed.
7. Get started today in helping others. (This extends you beyond yourself.)
8. Say a word of encouragement to others often. (Sincerely congratulate others on their successes.)

8.

—When I'm Sick?

Think back over the past three hundred sixty-five days. What has happened to you? I wouldn't be surprised if you were sick at least once. Perhaps it was a stomachache, or a toothache, or a headache, or, was it a pain somewhere else in your body? Perhaps you are sick now.

Two of the most respected physicians in the State of California called on me to discuss an imaginative and innovative idea in human care. The proposal includes on-the-spot treatment for body, mind and soul. Dr. Walter Buerger believes that the whole person has to have all-around health, and that if he is sick at any point (body, mind, or spirit), it can affect him at every point. Their plan is to treat the ailing in all three areas and at one locality—a Center for Human Care. Furthermore, they aim to get the sickly out of bed and on their feet in much less time than the average period of hospitalization. Both claimed that people need to get up and around, out and active.

Another statement got my attention when one of the doctors said, with authority, that sickness has become a way of life with some of us, and an accepted part of life with many more of us. Yes, drug-devouring and medication-conscious America has an abundant supply of sick people; not a sick society, however. This is the healthiest, most alive society on earth! I'm rather reluctant to admit it, but apparently this nation's businessmen lead the sickly parade.

Think back again. When you were sick, what did you do to lift your spirit and make you feel better? If you are ill now, what are you doing about it? There are three basic principles to guide you.

1. Health is holy, and sickness is abnormal for God's children. (It is in the natural flow of God to help his people be spiritually, emotionally, and physically whole people.)
2. When you are sick, you can participate, or be helped to participate, in techniques by which you can become a happier person.
3. By the application of creative methods to mind and spirit, many of your sicknesses can be prevented and the severity of them enormously abated.

One medical doctor said that the staggering bills accumulated through drugs, medical services and prescriptions can be cut in half, by working the third principle into everyday life.

How about the role of mind and spirit on your body in this matter of sickness and health? The term is psychosomatic illness —a sickness brought on by an emotion. It is also called E.I.I., meaning Emotionally-Induced Illness. Let's define emotion now as a state of mind reflected in the body by a reaction, either good or bad, depending on the state of the mind itself; for example, hope or despair, love or hate.

Dr. John A. Schindler, in his book *How To Live 365 Days A Year*, talks about Emotionally-Induced Illness. The doctor refers to a man who was widowed at the age of sixty-seven and remarried at the age of sixty-eight. At seventy-three, this husband was being treated by the famous Dr. Schindler for an extreme case of dermatitis. The patient never had any kind of skin disease before he married his second wife. The doctors found that upon being hospitalized, the patient would soon lose all symptoms of dermatitis, whereas within a week after being discharged and reunited with his wife, the skin would be terribly infected again.

The perceptive Dr. Schindler privately asked the man one day what he discovered about his wife on their honeymoon. The patient replied sternly, "I found out that she was domineering and dominating, and I just can't stand it!" That was the problem—a sickness induced by an unhealthy emotion.

A list of illnesses, with a percentage of causes by emotional factors, has been compiled by a group of doctors. Those physicians found out that 50 percent of ulcerlike pains are emotionally induced, as are 50 percent of gall bladderlike pains, 80 percent of dizziness, 90 percent of tiredness, 75 percent of pains in the neck, 90 percent of lumps in the throat, and 80 percent of all headaches.

According to Dr. Arnold P. Friedman, renowned New York physician, mental conflict is the major trigger of headaches.

The list goes on to include hundreds of complaints. From places like Mayo Clinic, Yale University Medical Department, Ochsner Clinic in New Orleans, and Dr. Schindler's Monroe Clinic has come the indication that over 50 percent of all modern illnesses are emotionally induced. "Doctor," I said to a physician whom I was seeing because of a pain in the neck, "do you agree with that figure?"

"Beyond a doubt," he answered. "Reverend, there's no question in my mind but that it's accurate." Of course, the sickness is real. Dermatitis is dermatitis; yet, why be sick when you can be well? Get the corrective measures to work inside.

We all know that modern science has a multitude of pills. A pharmaceutical manufacturer advertised a new drug in these terms.

> . . . a tranquilizing agent which places a barrier between the patient's emotions and his external problems . . . harassment and worry are replaced by an unfluctuating mood of untroubled composure . . . daytime sedation without hypnosis. . . .

Thank God for science and pills. Thank God that He has endowed and energized men of science to unlock the ancient mysteries of the elements which He gave. We all know that there are physicians and doctors to treat our illnesses, but we all should know that those treatments and pills are often temporary, stop-gap methods. What we need is the medicine of controlled and rightly-handled emotions. It is time for us to take hold of ourselves, with God's help, and refuse to take externally what can be achieved internally by peace of mind. You and I need to rebel absolutely from the slavery of dependence on pills.

Adjust! Grow! Mature emotionally and deal sickness a mighty blow! No matter what the sickness is or how it comes about, you can deal with it.

One method which has proven to be very effective is the program for spiritual self-management.

In our metropolitan region with a population close to one million, many people approach me about their problems indicating that they're bungling their lives.

A rather sickly looking twenty-nine-year-old man told me that he was absolutely chagrined with his life. "What's wrong with it?" I asked. Probably I should have demonstrated better Christian sense and asked him what there was right about it, because instantly he began to enumerate his helter-skelter condition.

"Frankly speaking," he snorted, "I'm a flunk-out at living— and at the ripe old age of twenty-nine! I've tried every gimmick in this gimmicky world; still, I'm a conglomerate of confusion."

When I asked what he wanted out of life, he replied that he wasn't sure. When I asked how he had lived the previous twenty-four hours, he answered by saying, "Just any way I could get through it." When I inquired whether he had any direction over himself, he retorted, "Mister, that's out of the question."

"Then," I diagnosed, "plainly you're suffering from a common disease basically of a spiritual nature. It is the old loser's malady. Your life is out of control. It's erratic; it needs solid management. And until you get it, you will fill a loser's image."

Not long before that, I had heard about an eighty-six-year-old woman who for seventy years had lived a wonderfully-managed life of spiritual depth. Her program for spiritual self-management had seven points.

1. Laugh at difficulties. (She finds they disappear.)
2. Attempt heavy responsibilities. (She finds they grow lighter.)
3. Face bad situations with courage. (She finds they clear up.)
4. Tell the truth. (She finds it more rewarding.)
5. Believe others are honest. (She finds that most of them live up to that expectation.)
6. Trust God every day. (She finds Him surprising her constantly with His loving goodness.)
7. Keep her mind on God. (She finds mental and spiritual peace that way.)

I wrote down these ideas and gave them to the young man. He has tried them, added to them and found them to work. The secret is simple. He is experiencing the phenomenal power of a managed life with spiritual roots; and, the equally amazing truth is that he is no longer a sickly sort of person.

This spiritual management for good health is the marshalling of God-power, self-power and strategy for the fullest life possible.

Another help which people have found to possess unusual preventive value is the spiritual commitment plan. It calls for one to commit his way to the Lord, for the basic question is, Will a person be well by the healing power of God? Don't scoff at the spiritual technique.

Dr. Andrew C. Ivy, that famed Chicago physiologist, said that religious attitudes of mind help keep men's bodies healthy. Attitudes such as love, faith, hope, unselfishness, forgiveness and tolerance set the body at rest and strengthen it physically. Antireligious attitudes such as hate, envy, jealousy, guilt, malice and vindictiveness put a strain on the body and are conducive to the development of disease.

Commit is to *release* by making yourself and your day available to God. Dr. Victor Frankl, the psychiatry professor at the University of Vienna, talks about logo-therapy. It is healing by the Lord. Many people could stand today in witness to the reality of God-healing through self-commitment to the Almighty. "Bless the Lord, O my soul . . . [He] heals all your diseases . . . (Psalms 103:2-3 rsv). God pulls out the sickness; God pulls in the health.

There is another idea for better health. Let's call it the life commitment plan: Trust God to help you work out your situations and humbly and reasonably to accept everything which proves to be beyond your control. Fretlessness is a proper word for this idea. Don't bottle up your day with fretting. Life has many turns and God is at each of them to see that you make it.

In the magazine, *Faith At Work*, the story is told of Annamarie Houston. She was busy at the bank where she worked as a teller. A husky man stared Annamarie squarely in the face, but he was fidgety as he leaned over the counter and handed her a note. It read, "This is a stick-up. Make no noise. Big bills first—or you'll be shot."

She didn't panic or faint. Calmly, she asked, "Where's your gun?"

"I'm not fooling, miss," he replied as he pointed to an object bulging from his coat. The man shoved a paper bag to her and said, "Put the bills in here; make it snappy or else."

Annamarie began putting bills in the bag. Still looking at him, she said, "You're in bad shape, aren't you? Upset. Worried. Why don't you talk to God about it?"

"Get the money and don't stall anymore," he demanded. "Besides, I don't know nothing about God."

Still she continued, "Listen, you're making the mistake of your life. This is something you'll always regret. Now, go on home and talk to the Lord Jesus Christ about it. Really, He's more concerned about you than you are yourself!"

The fellow looked at her, saw the sense of God's nearness she had (mixed in with a goodly potion of womanly determination), then wheeled around and ran out of the bank.

Annamarie could have fretted, but instead, she trusted God with her life; therefore, He would help her work out the dilemma —and He *did*.

Without adequately managing your emotions, you can waste your life. One can be led by the wrong leaders—those who thrive on animosity, hate, fear, envy and greed—when one is not in control of his emotions and feelings. He can be led to destroy, plunder, pollute, gossip and do all sorts of base things when he is not in control of his emotions and feelings.

A normally rational father loses himself in a fit of temper and beats his sixteen-year-old son. In a rage of jealousy, a wife accuses her husband of misconduct. Emotions, feelings—get them under your spiritual thumb. Be a take-charge person, by God's power for you, and rise a notch above the hectic snarl of frantic living. How can you become a take-charge person?

First, let the Spirit of Jesus become your Spirit for Life. Let the Mind of Christ be in you, as it says in Philippians 2:5.

Second, practice the law of substitution. It works in this way. When you are sad, think of something happy. When you tend to frown, crack your face with a million-dollar smile. When you feel mean, deliberately say or do something good. It is a fact that you will not be sad and happy, or frowning and smiling, all at one time.

Third, practice conscious thought control. Where are your thoughts this moment? Miles away? If so, they probably drifted there without your actually taking notice of them. Were I to walk up and ask you how they drifted, you would probably say, "I don't know; it just happened." The truly healthy life depends heavily on conscious thought control.

Control what goes on in that head of yours. Choose conscientiously what gets in. A man told me that he has begun to avoid gloomy, negative, pessimistic thinkers. I asked why, and he replied, "I don't want that stuff to rub off on me." Not faulty thinking!

In addition, activate your body, God's gift to you, as much as you can. Some marvelous results for better health can be yours! It has already been proven that physical work and exercise relieve worry and tension. I'm told that when a person worries, the upper side of the brain works more; when a person is physically active, the lower side of the brain works. Attention is diverted from one section of the brain to the other by physical exertion. Dr. Stewart G. Wolf, Chief of the Department of Medicine at the University of Oklahoma, enthusiastically encourages sports, exercise and work as relief for emotional stress.

71

I always encourage people who are sick to keep in their hearts the knowledge that the God who created them can re-create them. He made: He can re-make. As the Psalmist said, "Take delight in the Lord, and he will give you the desires of your heart" (Psalms 37:4, RSV).

Now, be still before Him. Release yourself to Him. Let go of tension. Feel the stress and strain going out of you. See yourself now as God's child free to live; see yourself as filled to the brim with the dynamic Spirit of the Lord.

THOUGHT CONDITIONERS FOR WHEN YOU'RE SICK

1. Memorize the three principles for healthier living: health is holy, and sickness is abnormal for God's children; you can participate, or be helped to participate, in techniques by which you can become a happier person, even when you're sick; by applying creative methods to mind and spirit, many of your sicknesses can be prevented and the severity of others enormously reduced.
2. A permanent cure for sickness demands more than pills.
3. What you think affects your physical health.
4. Peace of mind is the greatest physician you can have.
5. Spiritual self-management will give a boost to your better health. (This marshals your time and energies for effective living.)
6. Also there is unusual therapeutic value to spiritual commitment of yourself to the Lord. (This puts your soul in focus with your Maker.)
7. Add life commitment to spiritual self-management and spiritual commitment and your victory can be full. (This is to live with the facts of life and live through the challenges of life—by God's power.)
8. The product is a take-charge-person, and that is a healthy level of life on which to be.

9.

—When Wrong Seems So Strong?

"What are we going out into?" That was the question offered by a young man at graduation exercises for his high-school class. It has been my privilege to speak at a number of these ceremonies, and I have made it a point to listen to what the graduates say in their remarks, so I was keenly alert to the student speaker.

One bright young woman commented, "Our contribution to the society in which we live will be measured by the constructiveness of our actions." Those words are well worth remembering, aren't they? A young man who was at the top of his class, scholastically, but a cynic in his heart, said, "Let us go, parents! You've had your day! Now, we're going to have ours! We will do *as* we please, *when* we please, *where* we please!"

"Fellow-students," queried the third speaker, in a gloomy, dejected tone, "what are we going out into? There's hunger, poverty, destitution and illiteracy. This world is really messed up with war. Wrong seems so strong." He was right. Wrong does seem strong.

I felt that I could say with authority that men will carry guns until they learn to carry the cross; they will fight with their hands until they learn faith in their hearts and put it into action. We arranged to discuss the matter further the following day.

"I've been thinking of what you said," the fellow commented as he came into my office. "Wrong seems so strong; so very, very strong." I didn't put up any resistance to his statement. In fact, I replied that I agreed with him. Indeed, the bad is a powerful force.

I looked at him, "Have you ever thought of these words? 'He who is in you is greater than he who is in the world.'"

"And who said that?" popped out the young man.

"God did, through a fellow by the name of John." My guest was surprised to know that such affirmative, confident, positive, victorious and optimistic statements could be found anywhere in the Bible (I John 4:4 RSV). He, like so many others, had the impression that the Bible is only for those who are poor, or sad, or who want to marry ugly girls, live drab lives and go to Africa as missionaries. But he made an intelligent discovery: the Bible is for everyone who wants to *live* successfully.

"I've got to do something about my jobs," a man blurted out in my office. He was apparently so bothered that I asked him about the difficulty. "They conflict with each other," he replied. "I get twelve hundred dollars a month for one job and a thousand dollars a month for the second. I like the money; I need it; and I am competent in what I'm doing. But somehow I feel that I'm not doing justice to either company." One could tell that he was wrestling with himself, deep inside. To him, wrong and right were pulling fiercely against each other. But he, too, found help he needed in the old Book.

People of all ages face the same sort of experiences. I remember a little friend of mine who stood next to the display counter of taste-tempting candy. He had that Boy-I'd-sure-like-to-have-some-of-it look as he hungrily licked his lips. Being without any ready cash on his person, Chuck was confronted with a dilemma. Clearly, it was a matter of doing the right thing. Oh, how strong was the bad temptation to snitch a bar! About that time the manager walked by and said, "Trying to make up your mind which bar to take?" "No, sir," answered the wistful-eyed youngster, "I'm tryin' to make up my mind not to take a bar."

Tom, a rising young land investor and speculator is one of the brightest men I've ever met. One evening he phoned me at my home. "I must talk to you," he insisted.

"Tonight! I've got to see you tonight. Tomorrow is too late." We agreed to meet at my office.

A few days before, he had made a big deal which he knew was wrong. The proposition promised an enormous profit, but it took unfair advantage of two other men.

He sat down nervously in my office.

"I felt it was wrong," he lamented as he wiggled in the chair.

"Tom, you're a knowledgeable man," I said. "You knew that it was wrong before the deal was made, didn't you?"

"Yeah," he replied. "But I made the wrong choice. You ministers would say that I faced a tough moral choice and I cracked under it."

"Okay," I stated, "let's look at what can be done now." Although he couldn't back out of the deal, he could share the profits with the men he had taken advantage of. That called for courage, but he agreed to do it. Then we prayed, because he could get forgiveness and the spiritual strength to do right when he is faced again with a situation when wrong appears to be overpoweringly strong. God was there to touch him.

"I believe Jesus Christ is right here," Tom gleefully stated as he made a circular motion encompassing the whole office. "And," he spoke with assurance, "I believe He's right here," pointing firmly to his heart. Do you know what else that brainy young Yale graduate said? "I want to make amends for my wrongdoing. The desire is in here to do it." As he said it, he thumped his chest indicating that he meant every word he said.

The wrong yielded to love—the divine kind; God's love. It will do it every time when given the chance.

The one who is in you is greater than the one who is in the world. That means that through the Spirit of Almighty God in your heart and mind, you can overcome the strongest wrong. It is specific; it is to those who really want it. "You are of God," (I John 4:4). You have Him as your Life Partner. Your life is dedicated to do the works of the Lord Jesus Christ where you are. When you belong to God, you have *in* you the Spirit of mastery over wrong. Whatever strength wrong possesses, you have superstrength to overcome it.

I elaborated on this thought one day at a Lion's Club luncheon. After the meeting, a dignified looking, rather reserved business executive (whom I found to be an Ivy Leaguer from Harvard) asked, "But how can you be so certain about it?" Simply because God made you; because God loves you; because Jesus Christ is for you; because all kinds of people of all colors and ages have found it to work in their lives; because this case has an array of impeccable witnesses to it numbering well into tens of millions.

Three reputable witnesses to any matter is judicially accepted as conclusive evidence. To the truth that no matter what strength wrong holds, you can have amazing superstrength to whip it, there are irrefutable witnesses rivalling in number the grains of sand which line the winding beaches with a soft velvet pad. There is no science laboratory anywhere that can come up with any analysis more substantial than this one. Many have found words like these to bear out the offer of divine power for daily living: "All power in heaven and on earth has been given to me. I give this same power to you. I will always be with you" (Matthew 28:19-20 RSV paraphrased).

My teen-age niece, Charlynn Blalack, put it into practice one night. It was one of those beautiful, still Tennessee evenings, and Charlynn was bubbling over with excitement. She was going to the movie with her favorite boyfriend, a handsome, rugged high-school football player.

"Bye-bye, Mom," she said as she walked out the door. "We're going to the movie at the Ritz, and we'll be in by eleven." All of us were very proud of her. Along with the kind of beauty that attracts the eyes and whistles of every boy in town, she has a personality par excellence. This is a deep-rooted beauty, the kind that really makes a difference in one's life; the kind with which anybody will win friends and influence people.

Well, in a few minutes the phone rang. I happened to answer it. Charlynn was calling.

"Uncle David," she said, "We're going to the Upstate Theater. The movie at the Ritz isn't worth our time. It's filthy and it wouldn't speak well of Duane and me to watch it." Now, wrong was strong. The theater where the trash was being shown had many viewers, but the superstrength of right over wrong was at work in those two spiritually keyed-up young people; and they went on to see a wholesome movie, and one much more entertaining that the septic-tank junk at the Ritz.

As in Charlynn's and Duane's lives, so it is in yours: whether wrong is beaten in your life is up to you.

Dr. Viktor E. Frankl, Austrian psychiatrist talks about the last of the human freedoms. During World War II, Dr. Frankl was confined to a concentration camp and subjected to atrocities that took the lives of weaker men. His own family died in the gas chamber. From this experience, Dr. Frankl remembers a few men who walked through the shacks giving encouragement and their last bit of food to others. The doctor said that everything can be taken from a man but one thing—his freedom to choose his attitude in any given set of circumstances, and to choose his own way. The camp influences were horrible, challenging the last ounce of one's will to survive. Yet, as Dr. Frankl wrote:

> Even though conditions . . . and mental stresses may suggest that the inmates were bound to react in certain ways, in the final analysis it becomes clear that the sort of person the prisoner became was the result of an inner decision . . . Fundamentally, therefore, any man can . . . decide what shall become of him—mentally and spiritually.

Let this truth fill you today. You can overcome the strongest wrong, for through God, you are stronger than it. Through God, you are greater than your problem. A revision of a grand old hymn gets across the point.

> Rise up, O men of God!
> Overcome the evil things,
> Through heart and mind and soul and strength
> You can win with the Lord, your King.

". . . For *every* child of God," I said to the young man in my office, "is able to defeat the world" (meaning wrong and evil).

"I suppose that's from the Bible, too," the listener commented with a smile. As a matter of fact, it was. (I John 5:4, TEV.)

"Never thought of it this way," he remarked as he indicated his interest was aroused. Many others haven't thought of Christianity in these terms, either.

A man in my church told me awhile back that it is the most amazing discovery of his life. "I languished in pessimism, personal defeat, insecurity in my profession, and under the endless guilt of weaknesses and wrong," he said, "until the day it hit home to me that God wants me to be a victor in life. I'm a new man," he beamed. "Absolutely a new man!"

When condensed to its simplest form, the supremacy of a man over wrong is a matter of letting God in *and* letting God out. Let Him *in* by invitation and worship in your spirit. Let Him *out* through the attitudes and actions of a winner. Probably you agree that it offers an unusual opportunity for you to live in the winner's circle, but with every opportunity, one is accountable for his response.

I've prepared an account-ability version of "I Long To Be A Sinner," which appeared several years ago in *The Christian Herald* magazine.

I Long To Be Accountable

I long to be accountable for what I do. But I can't seem to manage it.

If I am a boy who copies answers from the student across the aisle, I find that I am only releasing some hidden inhibition. If I cleave my enemy's head with an ax, I am, in all probability, sick. If I run off with my neighbor's wife, I am socially immature. If I am an incessant liar, in all likelihood it is because my brother locked me in a shed when we were boys.

Like a pampered child, I can do no wrong. All my actions are conveniently explained by reference to the society which nurtured me and to childhood experiences which shocked me. There aren't any wrongs, anyway. Standards of conduct, like the spelling of *cat* or the way a sentence is strung together, simply reflect the custom of the time. *Right* and *wrong* are merely quaint ways of expressing what society, at the moment, approves or disapproves. My most serious offense (as any good marine has discovered) is getting out of step with my platoon.

Life on the topside requires one to be accountable, and that's good. I have been using a Creed of Accountability which shows how great this can be.

1. I am accountable.
2. Accountability make me strong.
3. Accountability helps me to accept opportunity.
4. Accountability motivates me to create additional opportunity.
5. Accountability sparks within me a creative fire for the good of those around me.
6. Accountability, in its deepest and truest dimension, helps me realize my need for God.

You are accountable basically to God and yourself to live stronger than the strongest wrong because you *can* do it. You can live stronger than the strongest wrong by *making up your mind beforehand to do what is right*. I used to get a lot of pleasure out of playing basketball in high school. In preparation for the games, Coach Bentley would gather us together for strategy meetings. During these planning sessions, we would carefully study our next opponents for their playing habits, weaknesses and strong points. We would map out our game plan, then when we went into the game, we would try to work our plans. Imagine trying to win a game otherwise! Imagine waiting until we got into the game to decide on strategy! But many people knowingly go into situations without much forethought, where wrong seems overwhelming.

Do you know what will insure success in such cases? Prior commitment. Make up your mind to do the right thing and no matter what provocation comes to you, there will be a reserve of spiritual and moral strength by which to overcome the bad.

To a sizeable degree, the outcome of the battle is determined before a shot is fired, because through your mind, you are predisposed to do right.

Somebody gave me some sound advice at a time when doubts clouded my mind on a certain project. "If you are *willing* to die for it," the friend said, "there is nothing you cannot accomplish." As my dear Aunt Ernestine often told her three boys, "Sometimes it is not those who can, but those who will." That's mind power.

I repeat this verse from the Bible every day: "I can do all things through Christ which strengtheneth me" (Philippians 4:13, KJV). *Can* denotes possibility. The wayward son said, "I will arise and go to my father" (Luke 15:18 RSV). *Will* denotes probability. *I will do it!* Fix your mind to do right, then to that, add want.

The secret is to *want to do the right thing*. There was a teen-ager who was always quick to do something for the church. He amazed me. If there were anything to be done and he got word of it, he would call up, offering his services. Oh, how I admired him. One day I asked what propulsion he had inside. He drew a card out of his billfold which read, BE EAGER TO DO WHAT IS RIGHT. "Reverend," he said, "that means to be full of desire to do good and right." Along with many others, he had discovered that desire will blow out the dirt.

Mix in a goodly portion of works, now, where you are. In other words, *do the right thing today*. When there's an important job to do, start on it right away. When considering the worth of an undertaking, take into account its value today.

There's an old legend about the devil wanting to destroy the church. Anger, a trusted lieutenant, volunteered for Satan. "I can do it," Anger said. "I'll make them mad at one another."

Then Greed offered his services. "Leave it to me," said Greed, "to make them devour themselves emotionally."

Jealousy said, "Oh, but Satan, I will destroy them through suspicion and distrust."

"And I," spoke up Despair, "will ruin them through pessimism.

I'll get them to believing that there's no hope, that everything and everybody is bad. I'll make them give up."

Up walked Procrastination. "Satan, if you want a thorough job done, leave it to me. I'll tell them that they have a great job to do. I'll tell them that they can do it, that their God will help them to be successful, that their future is golden and that nothing can stop them." Just as Satan was about to doubt Procrastination's loyalty, the disciple said, "And I'll tell them they can begin *tomorrow*."

To-morrow is the road to sorrow if you leave until tomorrow what you can do today. Make up your mind beforehand to do good. Desire to do it, and do it today. You will find that phenomenal inner power is yours to subdue wrong.

We have considered the mastery of a man through the Spirit of Almighty God within the man, and the opportunity with which this mastery confronts us. The opportunity to have the Spirit of mastery over wrong makes each of us accountable, but it requires a definite response on our part. What will you do today with your opportunity?

WHAT TO DO TO OVERCOME WRONG

1. Adopt I John 4:4 and 5:4 as inspirational verses you memorize or otherwise keep close at hand for instant power.
2. Condition yourself mentally to accept those two statements as facts in your life by repeating them at least ten times a day for two weeks, and at least once a day thereafter.
3. You can be sure that God will make them reality in your experience, for His ways aren't too hard for you (I John 5:3).
4. Really let God into your life.
5. Constantly let God out through your life.
6. Build up your awareness that you are a child of God by affirming your status as His child.

10.

—When There's a Decision to Be Made?

Everyone is required to make decisions. Some of us might have trouble doing it as did the man who was asked by the doctor, "Do you have difficulty making decisions?"

"Well," hesitated the patient, "yes and no."

In 1965, I found myself at the crossroads in my life. A decision was necessary in reply to an invitation from the oldest organized Protestant group in this nation, the grand old Reformed Church in America, to be the organizing minister of a new walk-in, drive-in congregation, which would be located somewhere in bulging Los Angeles County.

Would we try the untried? Would we start without a substantial nucleus of people (four families, counting my own)?

Would we adapt to worship services at a drive-in theater? ("Sacrilegious," someone called it—"Insulting to divine worship," claimed another.) Could we depend on the people to respond to such a unique concept of worship? Would I risk my ministerial neck on it?

It was a big decision for my wife Pat and me.

Decision was what the small boy faced in our Sunday school one day. In an effort to teach the lad a lesson in giving, his father had given him a quarter and a dime with instructions that one was for Sunday school and the other he could spend on his favorite candy. The decision as to which coin was used where was left entirely up to the boy. That afternoon, his father remembered to ask the son which coin he put in Sunday school.

"Well," said the boy, "I started to put in the quarter, but the Bible says that God loves a cheerful giver. I knew I would feel more cheerful if I put in the dime, so I did!"

Successful decision making for modern times demands the most resourceful ideas. It requires that we draw on the deepest energies available. There are more decisions to make over more issues, large and small, than ever before. Progress has seen to that. Have you ever stopped to consider that the enterprising man is confronted with many more opportunities for making decisions than the man who is at a standstill? If progress has a price, decision making is one of the payments.

One of the most impressive men I've met is Congressman Walter Judd from Minnesota. "Let me tell you," he said as we drove away from the airport. "I wouldn't trade my years in Congress for anything in the world. To be a good congressman, you've got to be on your toes all the time—in Washington and in your home district. It takes pinpoint decision-making powers, honed by the desire to do the right thing for your country, to the best of your ability."

A few weeks later, I told another congressman about my conversation with Walter Judd.

"Walt and I usually were on opposite sides of the political fence," he said. "But never in my life have I known a more conscientious and ideal-driven man. He practices what he preaches."

There are a few lines from ancient literature which reflect a great deal of wisdom for efficient decision making. That piece of literature is the Bible; the words were written by a physician, and they are well worth memorizing. Read them over ten times today. Think about them two minutes at a time after each reading. Something good will happen to you.

[Jesus] went out into the hills to pray; and all night he continued in prayer to God. And when it was day, he called his disciples, and chose from them twelve, whom he named apostles . . ." (Luke 6:12-13, RSV).

The decision concerned leaders. Followship depends on leadership. In other words, get the leader and things will move. A church in Southern California, and one of the biggest churches in this land, engaged a prominent polling firm to find out the reasons that seven thousand members belonged to that single congregation.

The church is connected with a main-line denomination. It has superb facilities (three million dollars worth). Its educational and youth activities are among the best to be found anywhere. Hundreds are enrolled in its multi-choir organization. All of these programs are of vital concern to a going, effective church ministry, but the pollster reported that number one on the list was the minister and his staff. That reason out distanced its closest competitor by a margin greater than three to one. *Leadership!*

The greatest investment a company or a church can make is in leadership. Investment in leadership is more important than in land and buildings—more crucial than investment in machines and merchandise. The leader will acquire all of these. An investment in leadership is an investment in enthusiasm, ideas, and other creative abilities, and these produce results. (To the corporation, they are cash in the production stage. They can be exchanged for profit. American business has a stock exchange. Why not have an idea exchange? This wouldn't be such a bad idea for the American church scene, either, in my judgment.)

Decisions on leadership have been necessary even from primitive times. The steps for decision making are basically the same regardless of the matter on which a decision is needed. There are five power steps for decision making which will produce amazing results on any level.

One is *quiet power*. Jesus found a quiet place where he could think and meditate. ". . . he went out into the hills . . ." (Luke 6:12, RSV). He remembered the Bible verse which has brought peace to so many. ". . . In quietness and in trust shall be your strength" (Isaiah 30:15, RSV). Decisions can be made best when your thought apparatus is conditioned by quietness.

My good friend Ford Marshall was on his way up in the accounting firm. Although the company had so many partners that it took most of the space on the door leading into the office to get them all listed, Ford's boss was thinking of adding one more— Ford Marshall. He was one of the sharpest young CPA's in the Los Angeles area, and the boss knew it. The day came when Ford was invited to dine with his employer. It was a very special dinner.

"Ford," he began, "You're a special kind of guy. Will you accept our invitation to become the *Marshall* in Taggart, Blair, Barker, Fry, Collier, Youngsma and *Marshall?* A full partner, Ford."

He was honored by the opportunity and grateful for it, but Ford had a life-long ambition to have his own firm—to start it himself and make it into something big from the ground up.

"No hurry," said the boss. "Think it over, and let me know when you make up your mind."

You can see the magnitude of the decision Ford faced. When he mentioned it to me, he had been considering the matter for over a month.

"I haven't come to a decision," he said. "We're at a stalemate."

I suggested that he and Marge (his wife) get off by themselves. "Do you have a few days?"

"Yeah. We can take a couple of weeks."

"Then get a cabin up high in the San Bernardino Mountains. (I knew Ford and Marge both enjoyed the high country.) Get to yourself and God. Let the quietness of the tall pine trees and the mountains soak in."

I was certain that quiet power would help Ford, and it did. They came to a positive decision up there.

Not everyone can go off for a few days every time a decision is to be made, nor is it necessry in every case. But each of us can prepare himself for decision making by being quiet for a few moments.

Think of the harvest. It is ripened by the secret, silent, invisible forces of nature. Some of the best qualities of life are matured by quietness and silence.

> If chosen men had never been alone
> In deepest silence open-doored to God,
> No greatness ever had been dreamed or done.

One of the best ways to condition yourself for decision making is to get quiet for a few minutes every day. Choose a place where you can relax completely. That quietness and silence will pour a healing power into your tired body and strained brain calming those frayed nerves. It will cure sensless anxiety.

Lord, help me to learn to be quiet.

Ease the pounding of my heart by the quieting of my mind. Steady my hurried pace with a vision of the eternal reach of time. Amid the confusion of my day, give me the calmness of the everlasting hills.

Break the tension of my nerves and muscles with the soothing music of the singing streams that live in my memory. Help me to know the magical restorative power of silence.

Teach me the art of taking minute vacations—of slowing down to look at a flower, to chat with a friend, to pet a dog, to read from a good book. Remind me each day of the fable of the hare and the tortoise, that I may know that there is more to life than increasing its speed.

Let me look upward into the branches of the towering trees, and know that they grow tall because they grow quietly.

Hush me down, Lord, and inspire me to send my roots deep into the soil of life's true values, that I may grow in your peace forever. Amen.

AUTHOR UNKNOWN

Another step to skillful decision making is *time power*. When you have a decision before you, give yourself the advantage of time. A friend of mine, who has made a lot of bright decisions on major levels, said that when he is in doubt on a matter, he writes down all the pro's and con's he can; he weighs the evidence, and then acts. He said, "You need time—just as much as possible." Outstanding decision makers, down through the years, have used time power.

George Washington Carver, the distinguished scientist and educator, followed a definite plan when making a decision. First, he did the spade work by attempting to find out firsthand all he could about the subject, then he would find out what others had to say. The great American would let the accumulated knowledge incubate in his heart and mind. All the time, Dr. Carver would pray God to guide him. "Often," he said, "like a flash, the answer would come—sometimes in the night, sometimes in my study, sometimes while teaching, sometimes on my morning prayer walk." Dr. Carver would always say, "God revealed it to me."

Allow yourself the blessing of time, as much as possible, but don't dilly-dally around and waste your time and talents. Make the time work for you. When the time comes for the decision, make it; then go on, and never look back.

The third power required for sensible decision making is *devotion power*. Stay with it until the decision is satisfactorily reached. Never quit! That is the victory of devotion.

Sports fans around the world have been thrilled by little Jerry Lindgren, the tireless distance runner. In the 1964 Olympics, as a high schooler, Jerry competed against the world's best in the 10,000 meter race. But in the trials for the 1968 Olympics, Jerry had trouble making the team representing the United States. A leading newspaper carried the headline in its sports section: LINDGREN WON'T QUIT. The writer was talking about the determined spirit of young Lindgren. The young man was bent on sticking to the tryouts until he succeeded.

87

Call it devotion. Proficient decision making demands devotion, and devotion is that commitment which stays with the matter and results in an intelligent decision. When you team devotion with *prayer power*, you are combining unbeatable devices for coming to a right decision. Prayer is very versatile. It's good for almost anything.

Prayer really puts power into masterful decision making. How? Because by prayer, you're in touch with Infinite Intelligence —Almighty God. His intelligence is shared with you only as you go after it.

Let me tell you the story of Mack Schulman just as he told it to me.

Mack is one of those unforgettable men. His two hundred twenty pounds are well distributed over a mighty frame. His face is set apart by a square jaw and a million-dollar smile. Mack looks like a pioneer, and he is one of the most rugged, American men I know.

Now, Mack is a top producer with his company.

"But," he said, "I wasn't doing much good until five years ago when I had the big decision to make."

"Big decision?" I inquired.

"Yeh—big decision. I had to make the big decision. Would I float along in life lackadaisical-like or would I fly high like any child of God oughta'? I prayed, 'Lord, help me to put all Your powers in me to work. Help me to want to do it, God. And, dear Father, I want to know where I can do this best.' "

Well, he changed jobs and started working and studying as he had never done before. He has a deep, radiant faith today.

"Back there," he said, "I flipped on power through prayer. I'm still doing it."

In one way or another, the experience of rugged Mack has been repeated in the lives of thousands of folk.

There is a fifth step important to decision making. It is go-to-church power, and it has to do with public worship each week. Through regular public worship, you share decisions with God.

Dr. Norman Vincent Peale tells about a man at the historic Marble Collegiate Church in New York who put worship power to work in his own life. The church custodian started finding wadded-up sheets of paper every week on a certain pew. The paper would have words like *sales office, new branch, Charlie,* and *sales force* written on it. When brought to Dr. Peale's attention, he asked the usher to find out who sat in that particular place and to bring the person to Dr. Peale after the service.

The next Sunday, a man was introduced to Dr. Peale as the one who left pieces of paper scattered on his end of the pew.

The famous minister took the man aside and said, "Say, I'm curious to know what all this means."

"I'm sales manager in the northeastern states for my company, and there are many big decisions to make. I've started sharing them with God at worship every Sunday."

The business man explained that the scribblings on the wadded-up paper were matters demanding decisions. Upon arriving at church, he would write them down, turn them over to God, and leave them there.

Every person needs the dynamic outpouring from regular public worship each week. It gives you a sense of God. It gives you a sense of community by throwing you in with others. It stiffens your moral and spiritual sense of values. It gives you a better perspective on things and life.

By taking these five steps, you are ready to make the decision when you come to it. You're set for action. Make your decision. Make it definite.

SPIRITUAL TECHNIQUES FOR DECISION MAKING

1. Make time for quietness. (Whether you take a moment or a month, it stills the mind.)
2. Take as much time as possible. (If you succumb to a hurried and rushed feeling, it may cause you to make a silly decision.)

3. Stick to the matter until the decision is made. (Decision makers and quitters are in different leagues.)
4. Pray about it. (Infinite Intelligence is yours for the asking.)
5. Get the feeling that comes through public worship every week. (Share your decisions with God in this way.)
6. Having made the decision, go on and never look back. (Lookers-back will run aground.)

11.

—When I Feel Worthless?

Many of our television programs are chillers, thrillers and killers; and sometimes the sets (as well as the programs) need repair. The repairman was trying to find the trouble with a set belonging to some friends in our neighborhood. A six-year-old son, who was watching the TV man in his dilemma, said, "If you'd clean out all the dead cowboys and robbers from the bottom of the set, it might work again."

Dialogue in a recent show included these lines. "If you died tomorrow, would it matter to anyone other than yourself?"

"It wouldn't matter even to me. I'm a nothing in life—a nobody. I'm worthless."

That's a real-life dilemma for many people. They feel worthless. I spoke to a college gathering in which I mentioned the importance of a healthy self-worth concept to future success. A young man pulled me over to the side and said that he was like a bent safety pin. "I don't fit in anywhere and I'm always sticking people in the wrong places."

Perhaps we can gain additional insight through the terms used to describe abnormal behavior. It is important to understand that feelings of worthlessness are related to fear. Some symptoms of such feelings include:

Exalted Ego. He tries to get other people to notice him, sometimes by aggravating methods and reprimands.

Hypocrisy. He works to hide his feelings of unworthiness through a veil of unnatural laughter, or as a put-on extrovert.

Domineering Drive. Rather than by reason and through inspiration, he attempts to govern others by a tongue-lashing or even physical abuse. He may throw out fear-lines. These are fear-thoughts, predictions of calamity, and forecasts of defeat to scare people into a response favorable to his own fear-flavored opinions.

Self-Affront. This is to take personally all unfavorable remarks and criticism. Oh, the misery produced in this person. In every conversation, he sees an affront to himself.

Relayed Responsibility. He is quick to blame others, quick to find fault, but usually he is projecting to them what is really true of himself, whether he knows it or not.

Stand-Offishness. He's a loner, avoids people and activities. He fences himself in; isolates his life from others; insulates his life from the "harsh, cruel" world.

Selfishness. He is easily upset and provoked, and if he doesn't get his own way, he says in effect, "O.K. Do it yourself. I'll be no part of it." Childish!

Thin Skin. He's touchy, especially to criticism. He usually reacts angrily to unfavorable comparisons with others (afraid he is being shown up).

Put all of these symptoms together in the same person and he is twisted beyond livable limits; however, seldom are they all focused intensely in a single person. Just one or two of them extravagantly at work in anyone is sufficient to produce enough wretchedness to kill off real living.

Take *Attention-Getting*. A man called me one day and asked if he and his wife could come by my office for a few minutes to talk over a problem that had become unmanageable for them. "Come on over and let's talk about it," I said, assuring them that it would be a pleasure to try to help them. (And it was a pleasure to hear from the man. In an overwhelming number of cases, wives take the initiative when there is a problem. They are the ones who phone and try to get the ball rolling—God bless them!)

About fifteen minutes later, two of the finest looking people I've ever seen were shown into my office—both of them about thirty-five years of age, I'd say. He had that all-American, he-man look. She was dressed so well that I was sure she had a place on the list of best-dressed women in the world. After congratulating him for honoring his body by keeping it fit and trim, I made reference to her excellent taste and dress.

"That's the problem," he blurted out. "She has a crazy obsession about clothes. It's not the money. We have the money to buy most anything we want," he added. "It's the spirit behind the clothes. Something is wrong. Both of us think so. Betty, do you want to talk about it?"

There was a problem, and Betty summed it up in the one sentence: "I go overboard on clothes so that people will notice me. That's it, I suppose."

The need for attention is basic to man's nature, but this need can be blown out of sensible proportions; then it becomes inordinate and unruly. Probably an obsession, as with Betty. Wrong ways and lavish methods are used to get the attention of people.

Grown-ups as well as kids do it. The child throws a spoon, bangs on the table, gets in every neighborhood scrap there is. Why? To get others to notice him. I have learned that we need to pay a great deal of attention to these children. Grown-ups have different ways of getting attention.

The body, clothes, cars, houses—too often we use these to say, loud and clear, "Look at me. See what I've got." (Add to it "and what you haven't got" and you have greed as well.) Acceptable methods, controlled need—those spell the difference between filling a legitimate, God-given need or an insatiable obsession (a personality gap).

There's a dynamic fact of life for you: God has entrusted you to yourself! You're the trustee of the most important piece of property in the whole world—*yourself!* You are a really great

93

piece of property, an individual with your own personality and uniqueness. You are important.

Emphasizing this basic fact in a sermon, I exclaimed, "God has made you important. There's no one else quite like *you*."

As worshipers left the sanctuary, a man with tears trickling down his cheeks took my hand and said, "It never dawned on me before. I'm important! God has made me important!"

The hard squeeze on my hand indicated he meant what he said.

He had a radiance of joy and sincerity on his tear-stained face I'll never forget. For the first time in his life (one that had been spent either running himself down or listening to others do it), he realized in his heart that he was somebody—God's somebody! You are somebody, too.

Are you going to let feelings of worthlessness punch holes in your life? Being a divine trust as you are, should you continue any longer under that plague of unworthy feelings? Of course not! The Bible, centuries old now, conveys some divine thoughts on this subject.

"In the Lord's name, then," wrote the Apostle Paul, "I say this and insist on it: do not live any longer like the heathen, whose thoughts are worthless, and whose minds are in the dark. They have no part in the life that God gives. . . . That was not what you learned about Christ! You certainly heard about him, and as his followers you were taught the truth which is in Jesus. So get rid of your old self, which made you live as you used to. . . . Your hearts and minds must be made completely new. You must put on the new self, which is created in God's likeness, and reveals itself in the true life that is upright and holy" (Ephesians 4:17-24, TEV).

It is abundantly clear that whether one lived two thousand years ago or in today's moon-magnetized age, feelings of unworthiness are a useless waste of time and energy. Such feelings are a pagan way to feel, and at the time of those feelings, one has no part in the life of God. That is to say, God didn't make you to feel worthless. As His child, you have a much better, higher and more enjoyable right. Then, "In the Lord's name," by His power which can be yours now, insist on throwing them off. That's strong language, isn't it? The sacred writing intends for it to be; for you must overcome your feelings of worthlessness or you'll never have the glory of a full and effective life! Unless they're thrown aside, they will become the dominating pattern of your personality. When this happens to a person, his life becomes a contortion of agonizing confusion.

Description of a character we shall call Mr. No-Nothing will illustrate this. Calling him Mr. No-Nothing has absolutely no connection with his intelligence or aptitude, but refers to his attitude. At one time, Mr. No-Nothing's life was full of no's because he felt he was a *nothing*. "No, I can't," he would say, "because I'm not up to it. . . . I'm not worthy of it. . . . I haven't the ability for it. . . . Someone else can do it much better than I can." And so on. People can go through life committing partial suicide by destroying their abilities, energies and creative qualities. Mr. No-Nothing was methodically doing precisely that.

After doing the little bit which he did, Mr. No-Nothing would wonder if he did the right thing. Almost every time I saw him, he proceeded to run himself down. "I've had a rotten day, but it fits the way I've felt. Wonder if I made the right move in that deal? Probably didn't. I've been doing lousy."

Feelings of worthlessness had so entrenched themselves in his thoughts (his consciousness and sub-consciousness), and his spirit, that they became the prevailing pattern in his personality. By his own admission, he was a miserable human being. When enough people feel worthless, they make up a neighborhood of No-Nothings.

One pathetic ailment is self-hate from which come those feelings of worthlessness. This self-hate expresses itself in two ways, by a *low opinion of yourself* and by the *superhuman hallucination*.

Dr. George Stevenson has often said that fundamental to good emotional health is a basic philosophy of faith in yourself; that is, a *high opinion of yourself*. According to the doctor, that faith includes a worthy opinion of yourself (not a low opinion); and the worthy opinion, if strong enough, will take you through stresses that otherwise might shatter you.

Without a moment's hesitation, I answered a caller threatening suicide, "You really don't think much of yourself, do you?"

It wasn't his life that wasn't worth living. Basically, he felt that *he* wasn't worth living. His sight of himself was aimed low. Here is a thought I hope you will remember for a long time. *Low aim and ambition is low self-concept showing itself.* Neither one speaks well of you or your Creator.

On the other end of the spectrum, there's the *superhuman hallucination.* This person makes no room for the laws of life. He acts as if he can do everything by himself. He treats himself like a dehumanized machine.

John had this sickness. After a big promotion in his company, John's personality changed. He became sullen and moody, constantly tired and worn-out. He became disinterested in his wife and children.

After two hours with a doctor, John was told that he was suffering from superhuman hallucinations. He thought and acted as if the company would collapse without him. As a result, tension and stress began to build up; it was evidenced through his work and behavior. In plain language, John was told that he was trying too hard to succeed.

Superhuman hallucination is an extreme expression of feelings of worthlessness. *High aim and high ambition is high self-concept showing itself, but fanatical (uncontrolled, unorganized, unplanned) aim is the projection of a sense of unworthiness being demonstrated through an utterly ridiculous workload.*

It is a popular idea for us to take an aspirin, or tonic, or a red-coated little pill to end these unworthy feelings. Medicine can do wonders for you, thank God; but the trustworthy old Book, the Bible, shows us the long-tested, the best and the most effective cure.

Get rid of your old self. . . .
Your hearts and minds must be made completely new.
You must put on the new self. (Ephesians 4:17-24, TEV).

There is one piece of this world which you can be sure of changing and that's yourself. These words were given to me by a worshiper at my church.

"Your task—to build a better world," God said.
I answered, "How?
This world is such a large, vast place,
So complicated now!
And I so small and useless am—
There's nothing I can do!"
But God, in all His wisdom, said, "Just build a better you!"

How can you begin today to change yourself and build a better you? The answer is to fashion a new self through a changed spirit and a changed mental attitude. By doing that, the feelings of worthlessness will be whipped. They will be replaced by trust, divine feelings and facts of adequacy.

There is an inspirational verse in the Bible which assures you of victory in your struggle against feelings of worthlessness.

God is our refuge and strength, a very present help . . . (Psalms 46:1, RSV).

God is (living rather than dead). God is (my own) strength (to overcome these feelings of worthlessness). God is (my) help (motivation—assistance to do it now, to do it right, and to do it thoroughly). God is present (here). God is *very* present (really here, close by, *in* me).

HOW TO BUILD A BETTER YOU

1. *Truth*. Everyone tell the truth. Be truthful with others and with yourself.
2. *Right use of emotions*. Get rid of all bitterness and passion. No more shouting or insults. No more hateful feelings of any sort.

3. *Honest work.* Start working and earning an honest living for (yourself).
4. Let your life be run by God's Holy Spirit. That's to let God guide you.
5. Live your life toward others in forgiving relationships, even as God has forgiven you.

12.

—When Bad Things Crowd My Life?

One Sunday a man asked me, "Have you ever met a man who pulls bad things to his life?" That was really a thought-provoking question, and a most unusual way to begin a conversation. He had stepped over to the side out of the line of worshipers as they were leaving the sanctuary. I saw him standing there, waiting patiently, and I gathered that he had something important he wanted to talk over privately.

When I appeared somewhat hesitant at his question, he quipped, "You're looking at one. I'm Mr. Calamity in person! Yes, sir, Mr. Calamity. That's me!" I invited him to my office for a few moments. He came to talk, too! "Bad stuff actually seems attracted to me," he said. "Like a magnet draws iron filings, I draw trouble. Like water flows downward, all sorts of bad things flow toward me."

He began his story, "My son was killed in a wreck. That was an awful experience for us; then, a few months later, my daughter got polio. While she was in the hospital, my wife tripped in the laundry room and got her back out of joint. She had three operations and got out of the hospital two years ago, but she hasn't been the same since."

This man had quite a story—one which sounded almost unreal. He went on. "A year later, my store burned down, and no one has ever found out what caused it. After we rebuilt my appliance shop, one of my drivers ran a stop sign and collided with another car. We're still in litigation over that one. So, I want to know, am I jinxed?"

This man is no superstitious fool: he is an intelligent business-man, educated at the University of California.

99

"No," I replied, "you are *not* hexed."

I assured him that neither the stars, the moon, a mysterious witchdoctor, nor any other hocus-pocus had a spell over him, and reminded him that in everyone's life some bad happens. Although he has made some fine progress, he isn't out of the woods yet. Over the years when misfortune seemed to follow him around, this idea became deeply imbedded in his thinking. It dripped into his consciousness and subconsciousness. A great deal of spiritual and mental therapy, along with solid doses of faith, are required to fully get him free.

Bad things happen to each of us, and if we are normal, healthy human beings, we wonder why. What are some root causes for them? Frame of mind is one. Your mind has very much to do with the conditions in your life, for the dominant concepts you hold in your mind affect your whole being in such a way that they tend to become reality. One becomes magnetized, you might say, by the ideas repeated in one's thoughts.

Jim Clark found this to be true. A man whose friendship I cherish very much, Jim is a high-school teacher and basketball coach. "Several years ago," Jim said, "I thought about speculating with some land. Property is a good investment in Southern California," Jim added, "and I knew several men who were doing quite well with it. But, I told myself, 'Jim, you're a teacher, a basketball coach and a student of the American Indian. You might know how to dribble a ball, shape pottery and perform an ancient Indian dance; but you better leave land invesment to the land investors!'"

He floated along in this frame of mind for awhile, then he took hold of his thoughts and determined to dabble in land, first learning all he could about it. He broke the I-can't frame of mind with decisive commitment. Jim began to *think* he could make a success as an amateur land speculator, and he *has*.

If sufficient in number and intensity, and if repeated in the mind often enough, thoughts will become living things. Thoughts attract the people, the conditions, the resources, the forces and the circumstances of life which are compatible with them. In other words, failure thoughts attract failure and success thoughts attract success.

Mrs. Yesterday brought to my attention the second cause of bad things. Mrs. Yesterday lived in the past, and her present was as botched up as it could be. Every success she talked about happened years ago. The many reasons which she gave for her present misery transpired in the past. For all practical purposes, Mrs. Yesterday's life ended yesterday. Now, she is simply marking time until her funeral.

There used to be a spy show on tv called, "I Led Three Lives." Some people are trying to live that way everyday. They bring yesterday and tomorrow into today, and they are very unhappy. I tried to impress upon Mrs. Yesterday the need to keep two thoughts in mind.

You can never regress to yesterday. Life moves on.

> The Moving Finger writes; and, having writ,
>   Moves on: not all your Piety or Wit
> Shall lure it back to cancel half a line
>   Nor all your Tears wash out a Word of it.
>   from *The Rubáiyát*

Keep the past where it belongs—in the past—for life in the past makes the present a pretty stale experience.

You can live today as a happy child of God. This is your day; there is no better day for you than today.

There is a man in my church who is now happy because he found out he could *live* today only by living *today.* He had let world events trouble him so much that his own thinking and outlook were defeated. (No one is helping anybody or anything when he gets to that point.) I told him that I could always count on him to present a gloomy picture of the day's happenings. People hated to see Harvey coming because they knew that he would inject a sour note into their thinking. But Harvey changed. What an amazing change—a reversal, a beautiful turnabout! Everyone who knew him could tell it. A deep spiritual revolution put him on top of the disturbing conditions.

"I used to mope," he confessed. "Now, I believe that I am bigger than the conditions. God has helped me see that I *am*, through His power." He has proven that he can keep up a cheerful spirit, whatever conditions prevail. Harvey's victory can be yours.

You can get your today going on the upward swing. These ideas may help you do it.

1. Believe that there is no day like *today* for you to live. (This will squelch all the miserable excuses that put a squeeze on your life.)
2. Get deep spiritual power into your life by trusting God for a really great and productive day.
3. When you wake up, say, "What a day to live, and I'm going to live it."
4. Recognize your need to live today.
5. Assure yourself that regardless of what comes to you today, you and God are more than a match for the difficulties.

Obviously, the biggest cause for bad things in a person's life is the *individual himself*.

As a boy, I wasn't known for backing away from a stiff challenge, but one day I got myself into a perplexng situation by provoking two classmates. They were as determined to win as I was, and those brothers were known in our neighborhood for winning just about anything they endeavored to do. Boyhood scraps weren't uncommon. Normally, you could expect to win a few and lose a few; however, none of us remembered when Glen and Bobby Cunningham had lost one. From the looks of things, they weren't planning on setting any new precedent the day we had our differences! Three ten-year-olds were just about to trade blows when Mr. Coffman walked up.

Mr. Coffman—what a man! He was the most popular teacher at Travis Elementary School, and he did his best to saturate our hard heads with enough arithmetic to get us on to the next grade.

Mr. Coffman was an unforgetable-looking man of the roly-poly sort. He didn't allow any generation gap to develop, although he was well into middle age. He didn't believe in a generation gap.

"Sit down," he commanded in his effective, coarse way, "and be quiet. Now, boys," he continued as his half-rimmed glasses slowly slid down toward the end of his ruddy nose, "we can settle this here or in my office with the brown board."

Oh, the brown board! Everybody at Travis knew of the brown board, especially boys of my caliber. It was Mr. Coffman's famed paddle which was carefully contoured on one end to fit his chubby hand; the other end had two small holes drilled through it so as to release the immense pressure created when the board made contract with the lower extremities of one's back portion. As for the color of the board—with years of use it had become a mellow tan, similar to Mr. Coffman's complexion.

That grand man always proved to be a very efficient mediator. We three boys, under Mr. Coffman's diplomatic bargaining, found a way to resolve our differences without fighting them out.

Clearly, I had been in a predicament. How did I get there? Though my own foolishness. Whether in adulthood or childhood, bad things crowd one's life because of one's own blundering.

A neighbor tried three business ventures which ended up in failure. After overcoming his doubts and fears, he started thinking of trying for a fourth time. "I want to get out on my own again," he said, "but I've got to be sure that I don't repeat the mistakes that caused the other three flops." I asked if he had honestly appraised the situations. "Yes," he replied, "and I know exactly what went wrong." Thinking that I could probably learn something, I asked him what went wrong. "Me," he answered, "me." You can't get any more candid than that. He recognized that more than any other person, he was responsible for the bad in his life.

This is illustrated in an ancient story in which the Bible speaks of a rich man who thought of his wealth only in terms of what it could do for him (Luke 18:18-23, RSV). The man let his attitude toward money keep him from a fuller life. Rather than make his life count the most, he chose to spend his life counting his coins. It is said of him that "he became sad" (18:23). That is a pathetic state of mind.

Sadness is not Christ's way of life for any one God's children. Christianity produces cheer. As Norman Vincent Peale said, "The man who says he is a Christian and who at the same time is fearful and gloomy and dripping with pessimism may be a Christian intellectually and ethically, but he hasn't much of it in his heart." This cheerful state of mind lightens labor, diminishes difficulties, and mitigates misfortunes. It gives a creative power which the pessimist never possesses, and it is a matter of choice.

There is a senior citizen living near my church who walks three miles every morning at a brisk clip. Occasionally we talk for a few minutes, and one morning I asked if the daily walk helped him very much.

"Sure does," he said.

"You do seem to be a cheerful man," I remarked. "My church is built on people with your spirit, and we'd like to have some more just like you."

"Oh," he replied, "my choice has more to do with my cheerfulness than my walk." He explained. "Every morning when I wake up, I say to myself, 'George, this is a good day. This is God's day. Now, old boy, you can be happy or sad. The choice is yours.' And I always say, 'Old boy, George chooses to be happy today.'"

In the same way that you can choose to be cheerful, you can choose good for your life. This is an answer to bad things. Fill your mind with faith, for faith will attract the good to you.

Bob Andringa is one who filled his mind with faith-thoughts. Today he is the sales manager for one of the biggest car dealers in the Los Angeles area.

Ten years ago, in what appeared to be a calamity, he was fired from the dairy where he worked milking cows. The next day, he walked into the office of the largest car dealer in town and said, "My name is Bob Andringa. I can sell cars. I can sell your cars. And I need a job." The dealer was so impressed that he hired my good friend on the spot. Since then, Bob has been setting sales records. "His possibilities haven't been scratched yet," one representative said.

You have noticed, I am sure, the faith that filled Bob's thoughts. Defeated? No! This faith gave him the courage of heart and initiative of spirit to tower above what looked to be a bad circumstance and conquer it. The bad was overcome by the good.

"According to your faith be it done to you" (Matthew 9:29, rsv), Jesus once said. These faith-thoughts will encourage realities which correspond to them—*good things.* On the other hand, defeat-thoughts will encourage realities which correspond to them —*bad things.* If there is bad crowding your life and you react with bad thoughts, you add to the bad. You increase the defeat.

The power of faith-thoughts is in what it can add positively to your life. It puts more drive into you, greater hope, more ambition —all of which lead to amazing achievements. It sends a person out to do for himself, and it draws to him the better elements of true success. To these faith-thoughts, you must *fill your life with good things.*

A distressed couple did this, with remarkable results. When I arrived at my office one weekday morning about 6:30, I noticed a car parked in the drive-in area. I walked over and introduced myself. "I hope you don't mind our stopping here," the man said. "My wife and I are on our way to work, but we've been having some big problems in our marriage. Lately, all the problems have pushed in on us. Today, my wife plans to get the lawyer started on a divorce, but as we drove by the church this morning, we decided to stop for some quiet inspiration. There's the cross rising up there over the sanctuary—the peaceful surroundings with grass, flowers, water, and birds. This has helped me very much."

As he glanced over at his wife, he said, "Mary, for the first time in years, I've talked to God this morning. I think we can have a happy marriage." She acknowledged with a nod.

I'm sure of it, too, for they began that morning to fill their marriage with good things. They had been coming to church on Sundays and a few months later, I saw the same couple in the drive-in early one Tuesday morning. He motioned for me to stop by. "We're still filling our life with good things," he said. "And life has got good."

"Divorce!" he exclaimed in shock when I mentioned it. "Are you kidding? Oh, we just needed to get our bearings straight. A divorce wouldn't have made us happy anyway," he declared.

If you cram in the good, you'll crowd out the bad. Both will not exist in the same spot at the same time.

I learned from a friend how to fill life with good things. He calls it the think-thank-toil plan.

1. Think good things. Fix *good* in your mind. Many assaults in our times will be made to rot out this good thinking, but the powerful Spirit of God can be in you to repel the temptations.
2. Thank good things. To thank, you must think. A number of people thank not, because they think not. Name your blessings. Talk about them. That will put a stop to complaining and criticizing.
3. Toil good things. Consciously, deliberately work at putting good in your life. Be a do-er.

Ralph Waldo Emerson was having all sorts of troubles trying to get a calf into the barn. Nothing he did made the little animal move. Up stepped an eight-year-old girl who put a finger like a hook inside the calf's mouth and gently led it into the barn. So impressed was Mr. Emerson that he wrote in his *Journal*, "I like people who can *do things*."

God motivates a person to do good. Work at it; toil. Do it. Toiling extends the spirit of *thinking* and *thanking* into fact.

There is still another way which is important to bringing good into your life. *Set up the good you want to have.* Let's call it *goals*. Napoleon Hill spent twenty years researching the causes for success among leading Americans. In the process, he had close contact with such notables as Andrew Carnegie, Thomas Edison and Henry Ford.

Mr. Hill's findings are published in the book, *Think And Grow Rich*. He reports that the most successful men have goals. In fact, one of the primary causes for failure is a lack of goals. Meandering without objectives leads directly to disaster; yet many people (as many as ninety-five out of one hundred) have no goals in life. They float along in humdrum fashion, working—sleeping, working—sleeping.

I can safely predict that the next year will be a desert in your life unless you get down to business and set some goals. Goals are projections which inject into one's life the combinations needed to realize them. In a sense, goals are advanced realities, much like bank loans. My banker friends know that a loan is essentially one's own money received in advance. Of course, your money in advance comes at a premium which is called interest! So do goals, and they require planning!

For goals to have their full value, three steps should be followed. One, be definite about them. General goals are no good. Know what good you want your life to be filled with. Know what you want to do and where you want to go. Whether you function as an individual, a Christian, a church, or a corporation, maximum achievement is possible only by having specific goals.

The second step in making your aims most valuable to your well-being is to be definite about your goals. List them on paper and in the order of importance to you.

Charles Schwab, the steel magnate, paid twenty-five thousand dollars for this idea: every night just before retiring, write down your goals for the next day. Set them up in order of importance. Time will be saved, more will be accomplished, and life will be more rewarding. Schwab found it to work amazing results. You will, too, if you will do it honestly.

The third step is to start working toward those goals. Many people miss out on good things because they wait for just the right time. Columbus never would have set sail for the New World had he been a tomorrow person. This nation's great Declaration of Independence would still be wanting signatures had our liberty-loving forefathers been tomorrow people. The spacecraft that carried our men to the moon would still be on its pad—or worse yet, never dreamed of—were our scientists tomorrow people.

Achievement and spiritual success is founded on today. "Tomorrow" is too far away. "Tomorrow" will cost you today. Start

where you stand. Use what you have. Draw on God's power. Get it,
if you are without it. It is *not* too late. Along the way you'll find
additional resources and tools by which to accomplish your goals,
but only as you use what you now have.

POSITIVE ACTION FOR GOOD IN YOUR LIFE

1. No one is hexed with bad things.
2. Some bad comes to everyone.
3. Your frame of mind will cause you to attract or repel bad things.
4. The past can bring bad into your life, if you let it.
5. Your life can be full of good things through faith-power. Fill your life with good deeds, and set the goals for the good you want to come to you.
6. Be definite about your goals.
7. List them in order of importance.
8. Start working to accomplish them.
9. Start *now*.

13.

—When Grief Overwhelms Me?

We need a creative explosion in the church—not the underground-church, rebel philosophy which some modern churchmen are urging, but a creative upheaval which brings on more dynamic service to modern men. After the banquet where I spoke about this, a rather dignified man approached me. I could tell that he had something serious on his mind. "Young man," he said with authority, "I'm Mr. So-and-So, and I have a question. Just how old are you?" I told him that I was born in 1936. "I thought so," he grumbled, as if that year were a bad one all the way around. "Creative explosion in the church, you say. H-m-m. The thought grieves me because I liked things the way they were. But," he admitted, "I know you're right." I suppose the creative explosion idea did grieve him, but not in the sense of being sorrowful over the death of a loved one—it was probably more of an expression than a feeling. Such is the case with Mickey Ray.

Mickey, a nephew of mine who has high hopes in life, had to overcome several significant handicaps to get on the football squad at Baylor University. One of them was his size. Any scout will tell you that he likes big, tall, husky, mean boys, but Mickey was hardly larger than the waterboy. His five-foot ten-inch frame and one hundred sixty-five pounds looked rather puny when he carried the ball into a defensive line of burly people-crunchers. "The bigger they are, the harder I hit 'em," Mickey philosophized. He confessed wryly, "It did hurt once in awhile."

Mickey's small stature wasn't matched by his brother, Gary Don, who was four years his junior, but two inches taller and twenty-five pounds heavier when they were nineteen and fifteen years of age, respectively. After one gruelling Southwest Conference game in which Mickey had been hit hard all evening, his younger brother, of bigger size, met him. Thinking of those teeth-shattering tackles, Mickey looked at his brother and said, "It grieves me that you're so young and yet so big, and I'm so old and mature, yet so small."

Grieved, he claimed. I am sure he was—if not emotionally, certainly physically.

There is a difference. The grief which we consider here is best described as a groaning in the spirit, such as sorrow over the loss of a loved one. It is an emotional reaction. It is a mental shock. It is suffering which makes itself known through the sense of feeling.

You can grieve successfully: grief is a Christlike emotion, and you can become a fuller person through grief. This claim is predicated on grief being handled creatively. Anyone who makes grief into a creative expression of care is also creative in other areas.

Thomas Edison was one of these creative people. On a bitterly cold morning in New Jersey, the inventor stood and watched his laboratory go up in flames. The plans, sweat, blood and tears of years dissipated in the rolling columns of black smoke. His son, who became the governor of that great state, observed his father during the fire. Edison was calm and quiet. The son asked, "Dad, what are you going to do now? Everything is gone."

Like the great man he was, Edison answered, "Thank God! Our mistakes are all burned up, and we can start over again!" A creative, spiritual person has the inner strength to take a shock and move ahead with it, as Edison did. The question is not whether you will ever grieve—for you will. This is an experience every human being confronts.

Probably you have met people who think that Christianity takes away grief—that when they trust in God, they will have no grief. Almighty God works *through* life's realities more than He does *apart* from them. The significance of religious faith is that it teams you up with God to tackle the hard realities and win great victories through them. Keep in mind that any religion which does nothing, gives nothing, costs nothing, demands nothing and suffers nothing —*is* nothing, *has* nothing, and is *worth* nothing.

Some of the best-loved Bible stories show the heroes in grief. Peter grieved when, for the third time, Jesus asked the big fisherman if he loved his Christ. Prior to that, Mary and Martha were grieved over the death of their brother, Lazarus. When Jesus saw their tears, He, too, was deeply moved in spirit. Jesus grieved to the point of weeping. One of the norms for our society is that men don't cry. "Leave that for the women," men think. The greatness of Jesus, a real man, was never more evident than through the two words, "Jesus wept (John 11:35, RSV).

During one of the darkest times of World War II, Winston Churchill said to his nation, "Let us so bear ourselves that if the British Empire and its Commonwealth last for a thousand years, men will still say, 'This was their finest hour.'" Those two words, "Jesus wept," describe His finest hour. He was all man, a tough man, and He grieved. It shows simply that the celebrated Galilean was one of us, one among us, and one with us.

A modern Middle Eastern king was much like this. In his heart, he was at one with his subjects. To get to know them and better understand them, he disguised himself as a wandering laborer and went out among the people of his kingdom. He stayed with one family for over a year. He lived in their earthen hut with them, ate the same simple food which they ate and worked alongside the peasant in his little farm patch. He laughed with them: he cried with them. After a year, the family discovered that he was the king. Befuddled and happy all at once, the peasant exclaimed, "Oh, you're truly a king. You have everything, but you're one of us." Jesus wept. One of us! One among us! One with us!

Nowhere does religion shine brighter than in the area of the *creative Christian philosophy of grieving.* The Master grieved because He *loved* (John 11:5 and 36). Love, the real stuff, is the only source for legitimate grief, and this love is the only lasting cure for grief.

Early one morning, I was called to a home where a young mother had passed away suddenly. "I don't know," the husband said. "This is hard to take. I loved her so. The children loved her so. And she loved us."

A few weeks later, Ralph seemed to be having the fight of his life. I phoned him and asked if I could drop by to see him. "Yeah, come on over," he replied. As we talked he reminisced, "I loved her so much, I don't think I can get over her."

"Of course, you can," I assured him. "Because you loved her, you feel grief. And because you loved her and she loved you, you've got to get over that grief." From his expression, I knew that he had never thought of it in that way.

Love caused the grief. Love pulled him out of grief. Ralph has since married a wonderful new wife. The kids are thrilled with her, too.

Often *grief is confused with self-pity*. To pity yourself is to sink to the place where you feel sorry for yourself; then, life becomes an excuse rather than a reason. Fanny Crosby was blind from birth, yet she never pitied herself nor would she accept pity. During a very productive life in which she wrote several hundred hymns, she would tell her friends, "Don't waste any sympathy on me. I am the happiest person living."

Hold on to sorrow long enough and it will turn into self-pity. *One form of that self-pity is stagnant grief.*

When Lincoln's son William died in 1862, the President resumed his duties; but on Thursday of each week (the day of William's death), Lincoln went into mourning. One day, a minister friend visited the President and told him that he was overindulging in grief and that it was unworthy of one who believes in the Christian religion. The wise minister also mentioned that the President, by continuing such an exercise in self-pity, was making himself less effective as a leader than a man with his responsibilities can afford to be. From then on, Lincoln changed and later confessed that happiness and usefulness, lost through his grief being turned into self-pity, had been regained.

You can reject self-pity, and you can channel grief into its creative course. "But," you say, "you don't know the extent of my sorrow." Maybe not, but I know that you and God can win the battle. You can overcome self-pity, you can reject it. You are capable of much greater thoughts than you actually think. You are capable of much better feelings than you feel when self-pity blankets your spirit. You are capable of much bigger deeds than those you actually perform. There is nothing to help you succeed when you always doubt your ability to succeed.

> If you think you are beaten, you are;
> If you think you dare not, you don't.
> If you'd like to win but you think you can't,
> It is almost a cinch you won't.
>
> If you think you'll lose, you're lost,
> For out in the world we find
> Success begins with a fellow's will—
> It's all in the state of mind.
>
> If you think you're outclassed, you are;
> You've got to think high to rise;
> You've got to be sure of yourself before
> You can ever win a prize.
>
> Life's battles don't always go
> To the stronger or faster man,
> But soon or late the man who wins,
> Is the one who *thinks he can*!
>
> WALTER D. WINTLE

Put aside every excuse. Sideline that little fox *if*. Believe that you can rid yourself of self-pity. Take the help of God in you, and you will take leave of self-pity.

Other than love, there are two well-known causes of grief. One is a feeling of rejection. It is easy to grieve when one's ideas aren't accepted. A hurt feeling is aroused inside, and one feels turned away. There is a way to overcome grief from this source. Learn not to take defeat personally. A historian said that in the Battle of Gettysburg, General Lee's army was defeated, but not General Lee—in battle the General was beaten, but not in his heart or life.

Several years ago, two boys lived in the same neighborhood of Abilene, Texas. They went to the same schools together, they played together and they went to church together until one of the boys dropped out, saying that church was sissy stuff. The other one kept going to church, developed a dynamic faith, studied hard and now heads a great insurance company.

His boyhood friend became a criminal and was sent to the state penitentiary. While there, he had a vital religious experience. Furthermore, he discovered that he is not the loser in life, but that crime is. In simple terms, he came to the glorious conclusion that he was not defeated personally; rather, the system of living to which he had formerly given himself was defeated. When he left that prison, he left as a spiritual and psychological winner. Today he is a leading citzen and businessman in a west coast community.

It shouldn't require a prison experience to convince you that to take defeat personally will keep you losing at life, even though you're an upright, law-abiding member of your community. A feeling of personal defeat brings on feelings of rejection which, in turn, produce grief. This is a wrong exercise of grief.

Another generator of grief is the feeling of irreparable loss—the death of a husband or wife, the loss of a close friend—bringing grief to the heart. In the final analysis, the irreparable loss is the experience of the irreparable spirit. *For every loss there is a corresponding gain.* The loss takes on permanence because the spirit won't accept healing.

Have you ever been in a dark room and pulled the drapes open to the big outdoors? Sunlight rushes into the room in the same way a gang of neighborhood children surges into the kitchen for cookies and ice cream on a hot summer afternoon. The room is closed in to itself until it breaks open to that which is beyond it.

Grief can be like that. The loss which produced grief has some sort of gain equal to it. By throwing back the drapes from around your heart and mind, you will discover the gain, and you will keep grief contained and creative.

We need to be spiritually successful through grief. We need to grieve creatively. We need to keep grief a servant. We need to affirm that we aren't the creatures of circumstances, but that circumstances are the creatures of men.

Some pointers can help answer these needs in your life.

1. Think of your case as common; other people have gone through the same experience. Human experience may vary in its mode of expression from age to age and generation to generation, but seldom is the content substantially different. So, when I hear of others who have had an experience similar to mine, and they won out, my confidence and enthusiasm are strengthened.

2. Ask God's help to beat off the temptation to feel sorry for yourself.

3. Make sure that you don't retail your sorrow. This will tend to increase it and to spread it.

4. Think of good things in your life. Keep them before you. This will keep you from becoming a moper.

5. By all means, never resign yourself to grief nor think that there is nothing you can do.

The teacher who looked over her roll book on the first day of school found the IQ's were sensational. Numbers like 140, 142 and 145 were listed with each name. "I've got a class of geniuses," she thought, so she tried some new techniques, challenging the class with work that demanded determination, will power, time and thought. The response was outstanding, the class did unusually well. It was when the semester was almost over that she discovered the numbers on the roll book were for lockers—not IQ's.

This illustrates the unrecognized and untapped resources a human being can have. You probably have some in you—much more than you ever imagined—and God will help you to release them in the time of grief. If you will keep these three inspirational verses in your heart in the hour of grief, you will tap those deep resources of power and calmness.

I will be with you; I will not fail you or forsake you (Joshua 1:5, RSV).

My presence will go with you, and I will give you rest (Exodus 33:14, RSV).

. . . be strong, and let your heart take courage (Psalm 27:14, RSV).

ANSWERS FOR YOUR NEEDS IN GRIEF

1. Take setbacks in the stride of living. (Remind yourself often that "in everything God works for good . . ." when your attitude is saturated with Him.)
2. Let Christianity help prepare you to handle grief. (It will not shelter you from sorrow, however.)
3. Keep grief buffered by love. (This will brush aside the superfluous sentimentality that nauseates any spiritually-toned person.)
4. Put a time limit on sorrow, else it will sour into self-pity and turn on you with decimating force.
5. Supply your mind with victory thoughts, for what you think about the condition that has brought you grief makes the difference in whether you grieve or pity yourself.
6. Genuinely believe that God accepts you. (This has eliminated that sense of rejection for many forward-thinking people.)
7. Accept yourself as you, with God's help, are becoming. (Commonly, people reject themselves, but this will lead you to self-acceptance on a spiritual plane.)
8. Look for a gain through every loss. (Expect to find it. Rather than give up or give in, search until you see it. Then thank God for it.)

14.

—When I Am Fatigued?

Jack Wheeler was thirty-one years old and a human dynamo. He owned the largest dairy herd in the area, and to go with his prize-winning cattle, he had the finest facility and the most modern equipment. Besides that, Jack farmed six hundred forty acres of rich, irrigated land. Every Sunday, he, his wife, Shirley, and the three children drove twelve miles to the city church. They also were there for evening activities and meetings during the week.

The most amazing thing about Jack Wheeler was that he did all the work at the dairy and the farm by himself, except for a part-time helper. I asked Jack about his day. It usually began at 3:30 A.M. and often continued to 11:00 P.M. Between the noon meal and the afternoon work, he always managed to get a five-minute nap—no longer, no shorter.

Most people wondered where he got his go. It took more than a miracle-working breakfast cereal or a tonic for tired blood! Jack Wheeler seemed fatigueless.

In simple terms, fatigue means to weary and tire. We're living in a fatigue-producing age. We are exposed to the pressures that generate fatigue. A doctor reported to a convention of physicians that this modern strain has a larger share in the promotion and transmission of disease than any other single condition.

The Lord is the everlasting God, the Creator of the ends of the earth. He does not faint or grow weary, his understanding is unsearchable. He gives power to the faint, and to him who has no might he increases strength. . . . They who wait for the Lord shall renew their strength, they shall mount up with wings like the eagles, they shall run and not be weary, they shall walk and not faint (Isaiah 40:28-31, RSV).

People bounce back from fatigue when they "wait for the Lord." They gain their rightful strength by waiting upon the Lord. The question is: What does it mean to wait upon the Lord? It means for us to employ every tool at our command. Every ability we have is from God; and the methods within our reach to deal with fatigue are from the Lord. We must not balk at putting them to work in ridding ourselves of tiredness.

Causes of fatigue include ill treatment of the body, such as overwork, overweight and hurtful habits. Wrong treatment of mind will bring on fatigue. An idle mind, a pessimistic mind or a worried mind will tire you. There's still another cause. It should never be overlooked that fighting God can crush a person with weariness.

Not long ago, a businessman told me that he wanted to invest in a venture which promised unusually large profits. The new company, however, marketed products embarrassing to a more conscientious person. My friend was a serious Christian. He wanted to invest, but inside he knew he should put his money elsewhere. The last time I saw him, he said, "I'm beat! I'm as tired as I would be after shoveling coal for weeks without a day off." Arguing with God and the right way will wear a person down in a hurry.

These causes have shown that fatigue attacks people on three fronts—the mind, the body, and the soul. The tools to be used in handling fatigue must be applied at the points where assaults take place.

Consider the mind. To deal with fatigue, you must learn to handle your thoughts. There's extraordinary power in your mind. Worry and resentment cause more fatigue than actual work. A man told me how he had made up his mind to hate language in graduate school. At the same time, he set his mind against butter-milk, the customary drink of the day in the school's cafeteria. The thought of Greek, Hebrew and German, which were required courses, upset his studies while the thought of buttermilk upset his stomach. After awhile, the young man thought, "If I'm to finish this program, I've got to pass the languages, so I suppose I might as well like them." Do you know from that day on, he did very well in his studies, language included! He said, "It got to where I actually enjoyed them." As for the buttermilk, he began drinking it to show himself he could do it.

We are well advised that what we think means more than anything else in our lives. Our thoughts have greater power than what we earn, than where we live, than our social position and than what anyone else thinks about us. Your mental point of view has no greater power to bear anywhere than it does at the point of fatigue. "Do not be like children in your thinking . . . be mature in your thinking" (I Corinthians 14:20, TEV). Mature thinking is to think strength. Think the very best of every person and each situation. Think clean. Think energy. Think faith. Think creatively.

To your mature thoughts, add rest. It was a fatigued Jesus who, after an arduous and demanding time of service to humankind, departed to the sanctuary of a secluded place for reflection and meditation.

Rest will bring strength and tranquillity to your mind. Within, it will calm the tired waters and hush the turbulent winds. Physical isolation is not possible every time you feel fatigued; therefore, rest depends a great deal on mental powers. By the use of imagination, go to the mountains and sit down by the trickling stream. Go to the placid waters of the valley pond. Walk along the beach and punch your toes into the moist sand. Stroll through the serene woods of the countryside. Listen to the peaceful melodies of the birds and chirping of the squirrels. Be still and know that God is God. This rest will put zest into your body.

Another way to get rid of fatigue is to properly pace your work. Hard, honest, aggressive labor is good for anyone, whether it be manual or mental. Overwork, on the other hand, is a disservice to the body which God gave you. Christ was very weary in body one day. Did He push himself recklessly on? No. He sat down by a well in Samaria and rested. In metals, fatigue is described as that action causing deterioration. In human beings fatigue caused by undisciplined work is that action which can lead to the grave.

One man boasted that he worked thirteen hours a day. "Good," I replied.

"Seven days a week," he continued, "and I haven't taken a vacation in eleven years. What do you think of that?"

"Where do you want to be buried?" I replied. The harmony of life demands that we set up a schedule for our work which recognizes our body as something holy. Take good care—God's care—of your body.

Once in awhile you meet someone with a special glitter, an inspiring glow. Ruth Bryant was a person like that. She must have a secret, people thought. How else can she get so much done, so easily? Ruth was a good listener, a troubleshooter, an organizer and a creative leader; yet, she never seemed tired or irritated.

Anyone who has been in her home knows the secret. It is shown by a simple, two-word motto hanging above her sink. It reads, YES, LORD.

Yes, Lord, as a way of daily life, will do more than anything else to keep you full of strength and energy. It will put the power where the pressures of life are.

RESTFUL MEDITATION

The quieting, restraining, healing hand of Jesus Christ is upon me now. He takes my fatigue away. His presence is with me throughout the day, and His presence helps me calmly and with control to meet every situation that develops.

15.

—When I Need You to Solve A Problem?

Problems! Problems! Problems! There's no shortage of problems, is there? The world is full of them, and people are always trying to solve them for *other* people. (Could that be the reason the world is so full of wrong answers?)

We're here to find right answers for the problems confronted in the process of *living*. Sometimes we might be able to help other people locate some answers, too. Ministers and doctors are in the business of problem-solving, if they're doing their jobs.

Dr. Jim Eiler is one of the really good psychiatrists I know. He told me of a problem-downed, sad looking character who came to his office one day.

"I've lost every desire to live, Doc," said the man. "Life has become too hectic and confused for me. There are too many problems. I would like to stop the world and get off."

"I see," answered the doctor. "I understand your situation. We all have our problems, don't we? But I'm sure you can get a new lease on life if you'll try. After all, life is like a trumpet. We get out of it what we put into it."

"Okay, Doc," muttered the man. "What do you suggest?"

Jim advised the man to start on a weekly program of counseling to include periodic talks with a minister. More and more doctors are including prescriptions of faith along with medicine and therapy. The science of medicine and surgery is complemented by the science of faith and the power of prayer. As Henry Ward Beecher, the popular eighteenth century minister, put it: "Half the spiritual difficulties that men and women suffer arise from a morbid state of health." There are tremendous healing and innovative powers in the simple faith that all things are possible with God.

When Jim made his recommendation, the man wanted to know how long he would have to come to the doctor's office and how much it would cost. "Maybe a year," he answered, and the doctor named the usual fee.

There was a long pause, after which the man commented, "Hmm-m-m, Doc. That'll solve your problem, but what about mine?"

Now, if you were God, how would you design a human being? How would the person you design mature and grow? How would you set up the human problem capacity?

Maybe you would have made yourself to look different than you do, and you would have seen to it that you have no problems . . . and still be alive? Here is the way I look at it.

Since I need not face any problem by myself, I can grow and mature through every problem. I need a great deal of help in facing my problems. It wouldn't do for the Creator to leave me to face life by myself.

I have found out that *problems are for solving*. Charles Kettering, who used to head up the giant General Motors empire, was an ace problem solver. They didn't come too hard for him. He celebrated when problems were brought to him. The bigger they were, the better he liked them.

"Problems are the price of progress," he told his chieftains. "Don't bring me anything but problems," he would say. "Good news weakens me!"

Many people act as if problems are for brooding and fretting over, as did a man who phoned me. "Oh, my," he began, "what will I do. This rat-race is killing me. I haven't had a break from a headache for over a year, and the pressure is getting greater every day." I learned from the caller that he was on the outer edge of the "middle-age press."

In his fifties and an officer with a moderate-sized company, the man felt the push of younger men on their way up. He was sure that sooner or later he would be pressed out of his position by the well-educated, enterprising "young turks." Many corporate officers in their fifties are suffering from the middle-age press. Like Sam they find it hard to keep a step ahead of the younger men.

"I've got a problem with this," Sam said, "a big problem. I've got to get relief from this tension and worry. How can I take care of it?"

I was happy to remind him that people in every generation have found ways by which to handle their problems, but regardless of time, the methods worked only by working the methods. There are three techniques devised for solving problems which have been proved successful.

HOW ABOUT SINGING THROUGH YOUR PROBLEMS? This is a first-class technique for solving modern problems. There is a story about Eric Johnston, former President of the United States Chamber of Commerce, and author William L. White when they attended a banquet in Moscow during World War II. As the evening went on, the Russian hosts sang about their country. The climax came when the two guests, Johnston and White, were asked to sing an American song. The two consulted for a moment and responded with the national anthem and the only other song they both remembered: "Jesus Loves Me, This I Know." The hosts were favorably impressed.

For centuries, music has been the common language of all creation. Birds chirp their melodies; leaves whisper songs through the gentle afternoon breeze; waters ripple upon the sandy shore, dancing to a tuneful cadence; trees whistle under the direction of the symphonic wind; and the sea wails as rhythmically as the most experienced orchestra. Man responds to music. Situations, conditions and circumstances respond to happy melodies.

If you want problem-solving power, get music in your mind. The singing spirit is more apt to come up with solutions to problems. Singing, alone, doesn't dismiss many problems; but it will cheer you up, and gird you spiritually and mentally to handle a problem with greater success. It freshens the spirit and puts optimism into your day. Without cheer and optimism, you have little chance against the problems of life. This is illustrated in the case of a man who was having trouble getting his day started right. He needed to get it off on a happy note, so I advised him to put some music in his morning—the earlier the better.

"I can't sing!" he exclaimed. He meant that by the time the sound went from his heart through his mouth, it was an ear-shattering noise. I asked him what he did first in the morning. He said that he washed and shaved.

"Then buy a hymnbook," I suggested, "and keep it by your shaving cabinet. Each morning, pick a hymn and sing as you prepare for the day."

He did. I understand that now his wife is awakened every morning to a rousing rendition of a hymn—"My Faith Looks Up To Thee," "Holy, Holy, Holy," "What A Friend We Have In Jesus," or "This Is My Father's World." In her own words, "It's worth it, after seeing the difference it makes in Mark's life."

The way to sing through your problems is to *see something in every problem which you can sing about*. Some people scowl and growl when problems come to them. Anyone with this sort of spirit is his own biggest and most perplexing problem. The mind put to song actually is more receptive to problem-solving ideas.

So your problem *is* a big one. It looks like a dark one, but you can put some light into it. Find *something* in it to sing about. Probe, dig, search, if you have to, but find *something*. You'll find it if you want to.

A man in high government circles has ample opportunity to show his problem-solving finesse. There are plenty of problems! One of these officials faces many problems, but he is able to handle them because his grand, old mother had enough self-taught education and solid Christian optimism to teach him a valuable lesson early in life. She instilled in him the life-building, problem-answering idea that no problem is best met with a sour note.

In his early years, he complained to his mother about their hardships. Things were meager, clothes were hand-me-downs, and there was hardly enough food to go around.

"Now, look here, young man," that good woman insisted. "I've given you life. I wish I could give you much more, but at least I've given you life, and that's the best I have. Now you stop your complaining and get out and do something with it!" This is the sound advice which more parents need to give their kids in our day of plenty.

Another valuable course to take in solving that problem is to TALK OVER THE PROBLEM WITH GOD. This is prayer.

Dan can tell you that it works. He is one of the brightest teen-agers I have the joy of knowing. Sitting around the supper table one evening, Dan told his mother and father that for the first time in his life, he realized he could take his problems to God and talk them over with the Almighty.

Everyone of God's children ought to realize this and do it. You don't embarrass God. No problem of yours insults Him, and you shouldn't be embarrassed about it.

"I feel at ease, now," Dan said, "in taking my problems to God. I am comfortable doing it. And the results! Boy, does it do something for me! It does something THROUGH ME to the problems!"

Teen-agers have big problems these days, just as big and real as any problem they'll have when they're fifty. But as Dan made crystal clear, prayer helps him to know what to do, and through prayer, he finds added zest to do it. This can be true for you.

Prayer is a big plus factor in solving problems because at least three great things happen when you talk to God honestly and sincerely about your problems.

One: Prayer helps you listen while God speaks. Oh, how we need to listen to the Almighty. There is wisdom and power equal to any problem available to you through Him. You can tap them only by keeping open the channel of your spiritual inner ear. This is done by prayer.

Two: Through prayer, you get yourself attuned to God. The spiritual, emotional, mental and physical self will get on the same exhilarating level, if you make a practice of honest and open prayer.

Three: Through this kind of prayer (which is the only kind of real prayer), you get your whole self synchronized as a unified force, working together as one unit for the good of the whole.

The biggest problems will melt under the dynamic heat generated by these prayers from enthusiastic, thankful, determined people. How successful are you with that nagging problem? Are you ready to try prayer? Do it. Seek the help of a qualified spiritual counselor —a minister, priest, or rabbi—to help you, if you feel a need for some assistance in getting started.

In our accelerated, moon-magnetized society, some people have even said that today's man is too sophisticated to try prayer. Prayer is said to be unscientific, but the science of prayer has been proven many times.

What Henry Ford did for the American automobile, William James did for the social sciences in our great land. On one occasion, the Harvard professor discussed prayer and its scientific validity. "We hear in these days of scientific enlightenment a great deal of discussion about the efficacy of prayer, and many reasons are given us why we should not pray, whilst others are given why we should. . . . The reason why we do pray is simply that we cannot help praying."

Glenn Clark, the respected educator, speaks of the science of prayer in these words. "Prayer is governed by the same laws that govern the growth of the flower in the crannied wall. It is controlled by the same laws that control the flow of a stream, for, as God is in all things, so are his laws prevailing in all things."

Dr. Clark added, "As prayer is life raised to the highest degree, so the laws of prayer are the laws of life raised to their highest expression."

He demonstrated penetrating, practical vision on the scientific acceptability of prayer when he said, "The man who learns and practices the laws of prayer should be able to play better, to work better, to love better, to serve better, for to learn how to pray is to learn how to live."

A group of businessmen met for breakfast to talk about "Prayer-Power For Modern Problem-Solving." Of great significance was the story told by Charles Martin, who owned a chain of supermarkets on the West Coast.

"One time," Chuck said, "I read of a man who was too busy to be in a hurry. If he allowed himself to get in a hurry, he couldn't do everything which he had to do." The astute businessman went on to say that he is too busy to be in a hurry.

"My experience has proven that when I get in a hurry my mind becomes clogged-up. Decisions and problem-solving then come hard for me. But the secret for me is to keep busy, yet not hurried, and to really solve problems is no secret at all. It's prayer."

Problem-solving prayer is more than a neat compilation of flowery words. It's from the heart! It expresses the deepest throbbing of the mind. This holds true for corporate prayer as well.

What an experience we had in Covington, Tennessee! While visiting the area as vacationers, my wife and I quietly slipped in to the Methodist Church for the Sunday service. We've learned to take God *with* us on vacation. It adds something to the rest and relaxation.

For close to one hundred fifty years, this church has been telling people of God's love. Many have prayed and listened to prayers inside its stately old sanctuary, but I am sure that no greater prayer has ever been offered from its pulpit than the one we shared that Sunday. The whole worship service was very inspiring, but it was immensely enhanced by the morning prayer.

A layman led us in the prayer. He talked to God as a contemporary to a Contemporary. He talked to God as one living to One living. He talked as one who knew about problems to One who, for thousands of years, has shown keen expertise in helping people find answers to them. He talked from the soul out, covering personal, group and community problems. No superficiality there! No meaningless, pious, paltry chatter. Prayers like that churn up solutions! The experience will live long in our hearts.

Prayer really works as a problem solver for *everyone* who dares to engage himself in it honestly and consistently, and who backs it up with words and deeds which prayer inspires.

There is another substantial problem-solving power which comes to you in the form of deeply entrenched belief. BELIEVE THROUGH YOUR PROBLEM. Anchor your spirit like a mighty foundation with the belief that you can and will get through the problem, and remember that God is in there with you—not "out there somewhere," away from you—to help pull you through. With belief like that, anybody can sing through his problem. The amazing truth is that *anybody can have a belief like that.*

Terrie Hamilton has belief that pushes her problem around. The first thing I saw after walking into her lovely home was a bronze plaque which read: ATTITUDE IS MORE IMPORTANT THAN FACT. I was soon to find it out.

"Be with you in a minute, Reverend," came a voice from a rear room. Terrie came out laboriously handling her wheel chair. Terre has had multiple sclerosis for the past twenty years. Although unable to walk on her legs for these many years, she walks in her soul.

"Reverend, I wouldn't miss church for anything in this world." She has difficulties getting awake and around on other mornings, but on Sunday Terrie is the first one up.

"I'm like the old town crier," she said. "At the break of dawn, I'm up and knocking on Bill's and Mother's doors, and I say, 'Come on now, it's time to get up for church. We don't want to be late. Up, up, up, let's go!'"

Just about the time I was wondering how she maintained that royal spirit through the years, Terrie said, "I pray a lot, Reverend. I talk to God like He's here by me. And He is," she insisted. "Jesus Christ is right here in this room now."

No one else was visible in that room—but God was there. I knew it.

"Reverend," Terrie commented, "I read all I can in the Bible, too. Oh, inspirational materials have been a lifesaver to me. I have books; look at 'em on my bookshelf. I have your sermons, as well," she said. Her belief sweeps through problems, even dark ones, with problem-solving light. The psalm might be paraphrased to read:

Happy is everyone who is strong in the Lord, in whose heart are the ways of God. Passing through the valley of weeping, they regard it a place of springs; it is covered with blessings. . . . They go on from strength to strength . . . (Psalms 84:5-7, RSV).

A very worried, problem-plagued man took that verse, committed it to memory, repeated it ten times each day for thirty days, meditated each day on what it meant to him, affirmed it as his experience and it changed his life. Why don't you do the same? Anybody can have belief like that. Of course you can! How much do you want it?

You can have it, for ". . . When you pray and ask for something, believe that you have received it, and everything will be given you" (Mark 11:24, TEV).

SPIRITUAL TECHNIQUES FOR PROBLEM SOLVING

1. Spiritual techniques and medical science produce spiritually, mentally, emotionally and physically vibrant people.
2. Your problems *can* be solved.
3. Approach those problems with a singing spirit. (This will better fit you for solving them.)
4. Find something in *every* problem which you can genuinely sing about.
5. Apply prayer to your problems.
6. God listens to you because He has a vested interest in you. (He created you!)
7. Apply belief, the deep stuff, to your problems.
8. If you really want answers to your problems, you can find them. (It is a case of: Will you go after those solutions?)

16.

—When the Unpredictable Happens?

One of the sturdiest men anywhere is Tom Hanks, my wife's uncle. He isn't afraid of a challenge nor does he back off from work. Tom takes a lot of pride in being a first-rate farmer of some six hundred acres in western Tennessee, and his herd of more than five hundred cattle gets the deluxe TLC (Tender Loving Care) treatment. They never had it so good.

Farming is a science and any science has laws and principles. Plant right and on time. Tend the crops properly. Take care of the soil. Harvest at the right time. Tom can count on the law of planting, tending and harvesting to bring him a good yield.

There are unpredictable elements—a wash-out, or a drought, or a windstorm, or a hailstorm. Sometimes, in a matter of minutes, a whole crop is wiped out in a single avalanche of hailstones. Everywhere you go you will find some unpredictable happenings in life.

Tragedy suddenly strikes a young family, leaving a wife and three children without a husband and father. Sickness requires major surgery and a drawn-out period of convalescence. The breadwinner loses his job. Without warning, a bright and cheerful child is quickly taken from a couple. To the surprise of the family, a man takes his own life. A woman is arrested on a narcotics charge. A promising teen-ager abruptly turns to an unprincipled way of life. There is a victory—sometimes in subtle form—to be gained when the unpredictable happens.

A young man went to work as a box boy in a grocery store after he was graduated from high school. He liked the job very much, and after a few weeks of work, the young man's dad said, "It's time now to talk about your college education, son."

"College?" queried the son. "Oh, Dad, I guess I didn't tell you. I've decided not to go to college."

"What do you mean you're not going to college? If you apply yourself at school, after you get that degree, there's no limit to what you can do."

"Dad, I've found my life's work there as a box boy. I'm quick at putting those groceries into the sacks. I keep the counters clean, and I'm going to be the best box boy in the store. I've found my niche, Dad, and I'm going to stay there."

After thinking it over, the boy's father went to the store and told the manager that he would have to fire his son.

"Why should I fire him? He's the best box boy in the store!"

"Well," answered the father, "he has decided he doesn't need to go to college because of his job here."

When Saturday night rolled around, the manager called the young man into his office and said, "You're fired."

"What happened?"

"You're fired."

"What's wrong?"

"You're fired."

"Wh---?"

"You're fired!"

The young man got the impression he was fired. He hadn't expected it. It was sudden. It was one of the unpredictable turns in his life.

All the way home, he thought about it. His spirit was at an all-time low. When the boy got home, he said: "Dad, I'm going to college." Twenty years later and still in his thirties, the man was selected as president of a great university. Soon after, he wrote to his old boss and said, "Thanks for firing me." The fact that his father engineered it remained a secret between him and the grocer until the father passed away.

Long ago, Jesus was well aware of the unpredictability in life, and for that reason He taught that you need not worry about what is going to happen. Instead, concern yourself with what *is* going on.

"So do not worry about tomorrow; it will have enough worries of its own. There is no need to add to the troubles each day brings" (Matthew 6:34, TEV). Yet, we usually want to see what will happen, much like the editor during the French Revolution. As he was being locked in the guillotine about to be beheaded, he said, "It's too bad to take my head off now. I really wanted to see how this thing is coming out." Most of us are like that when it comes to life.

"Take the unpredictability out of my life and I'll do better," we think. Really? Some leading doctors disagree. "We'd go insane if we actually knew everything which is going to happen to us for the next year," Dr. Robert Dukes of Pomona, California, said to me. "Our Creator has done a good job in making us take life as it comes."

Even though you don't know everything that will happen in your future, you can prepare yourself generally for it. *Preparation* is the secret to facing the unpredictable with confidence and calmness.

Mr. Share is a man who has made preparations to share himself with the world in any eventuality. One morning about two years after Mr. Share joined my church, I received an envelope which had been mailed from the Los Angeles Airport. Inside was a will—written out in longhand, dated, and signed—and an insurance policy.

Mr. Share, in his thirties, had an estate amounting to about two hundred thousand dollars, most of which is insurance. He had spelled out the distribution of it in case of his demise.

"Ten percent to Valley Community Drive-In Church."

He put this first in his will. Mr. Share is an avid tither. He gives at least 10 percent of his income to the church. Since beginning to tithe two years ago, he averages over fifteen hundred dollars a year in donations to the church. His income is now about fifteen thousand dollars.

"Mary and I wouldn't have it any other way," he told me privately. "We have found that it adds so much to our lives, and our church means so much to us. We can never repay the good it has done for us." These are the words of a layman—who shares!

Isn't it encouraging that a church can make such a difference to a couple? And skeptics say the church is on its way out! Truth, when presented positively, and in such a way that it helps people to live happily day-by-day, blended with enthusiasm, in a church where God is really alive, will produce wondrous results! There is no limit to the good people will do in and for such a church!

To the 10 percent clause, Mr. Share added, "The remainder goes to my wife." In that envelope there was also a policy which Mr. Share had taken out before he boarded the plane. It was flight insurance in the amount of fifty-two thousand, five hundred dollars made out to the church. Attached was a note.

"I want to share in my church's dynamic work when I'm gone."

This has become a regular practice for Mr. Share since then. Every time he goes away, I get an insurance policy from the airport. What a man! His example is good for every one of us.

Mr. Share demonstrates preparation. You don't know the future, yet you can prepare for whatever the future brings.

The seemingly invincible Vince Lombardi is the most successful professional football coach of modern times. As a superb motivator of men, Lombardi acknowledged the importance of preparation. He used to tell his tough squad that if they were confident, they would be apt to do their best, and if they were prepared, even for the unexpected, they would not be jolted, even by the unexpected.

This *preparation* must be taken literally. It is to make ready beforehand. To wait for the situation without having laid as sound a foundation as possible is like having a wedding without an engagement. It is like proposing marriage without having met the girl.

This preparation depends a great deal on the power of expectation. The prefix *ex* means *out; pect* has Latin origins meaning *to look.* Handling the unpredictable with ease takes a condition of the heart and mind involving both faith and attitude. To be prepared for the unpredictable, you combine faith with a spiritual drive and the product in the moment of surprise will be a great victory. When this immense power is positively put to action in you, the harshest occurrence can be turned into a victory.

There is a legend about a German baron who built a huge castle on the Rhine River. From corner to corner, he strung wires in an effort to get music from winds as they blew across those wires. For a long time, he waited, but there was no music. The winds blew, but they were not strong enough to make music.

Finally a ferocious storm stirred the mighty Rhine from bank to bank. Lightning creased the black skies like a searing hot iron. Thunder rolled as mighty drums, and the earth trembled under its roar. With a madness, the winds whipped across his harplike wires. Music—there was the sound of music. The baron stood by a window and watched the terrifying storm as he listened to heavenly music. At last, a powerful tempest had brought music out of the wires.

This is experienced in real life by many people. Not expecting a revolting development, they rise up with enthusiasm and make music to it, when it comes. To do this, be a take-charge person and *expect to handle any situation.*

It has been proven that we act and react according to our sense of what we expect of ourselves; and, in some respects, our response is conditioned by what we believe others expect of us. Do you expect yourself to take charge of the predicaments in your life? Others can expect it of you, but you will never make it happen until you expect it of yourself. Is your expectation powerful? Exercise it every day and it will grow into a power-packed reality. It needs to be a growing expectation if you are to handle surprise situations with skill and ease.

Expect to give thanks. A family in New York had a hard time living up to this idea, but they made it. Their day off almost became an off day. It was planned as a day off for sightseeing, shopping, relaxation, fun and eating out as a family. The morning began with a wind of almost gale proportions howling against the windows. Soon, sheets of rain poured down on the earth.

The day off became an off day until the six-year-old daughter taught them a valuable lesson. After a breakfast marked by disappointment and dejection, the small girl went to her room. As Mother passed by, she heard her tot pray, "Dear God, thank you for the pretty flowers and grass we're gonna have when all the rain stops." That is gratefulness through the unpredictable turns in life.

Every one of us can give thanks when the unpredictable happens. This is no bit of ivory-tower advice. It is practical and realistic. Whatever the event, there's enough good and right for which to sincerely tell God, "Thank You." The most successful people in every age have found it to be so. This variety of realism consists of adding a buoyant spirit of gratitude to the hard realities of life. The trouble is that many of us do not look for the good in the unpredictable when it happens. Defeatism scourges us into submission until gloom floods our thoughts and feelings.

There is a fourteen-year-old boy in my neighborhood who lost two fingers in a lawn mower accident. "Oh, my goodness!" lamented the people when they saw his bandaged hand. "Isn't it terrible?"

The young fellow expressed more adult gumption than some of the adults when he said, "They keep crying over the two lost fingers, but never stop to think that I still have three good ones left on the same hand."

Put a small black dot on a sheet of white paper and ask people what they see. This is a revealing experiment which shows attitudes and patterns of life. Usually they will see the infinitesimal black dot; not the sea of whiteness around it. When I did this experiment recently, 95 percent of the people—adult, educated, intelligent human beings—mentioned the black dot (no larger than a pin point) which I had on 36 x 48 inches of solid white cardboard.

At a personnel manager's convention, two men from giant companies spoke of evaluation programs for executives. The objective was to increase an executive's assets to the company and decrease his liabilities. One of the men referred to it as defects whereas the other spoke of it as excellence achievement. One was negative; the other was positive. One saw the small black dot; the other saw the large white cardboard.

The secret in giving thanks when the unpredictable happens is: search out the good and enumerate it. Think on it. Size it up in comparison with how bad it could have been. Another idea is to let the power of expectation build up faith that *God will be your close companion* in every unpredictable situation.

Alexander Maclaren discovered what divine companionship is all about when he accepted his first job at the age of sixteen. It was in the city of Glasgow, Scotland, six miles from home. Between home and the city there was a deep ravine which, according to popular reports, was haunted. All sorts of terrible things happened in that ravine, people in those parts had been told.

On Monday morning Alex left for the week of work, and father Maclaren walked with his son to the job. "Alex," he said in leaving, "come home as fast as you can when you get off Saturday night."

Thinking of the ravine, the young man replied, "But, Dad, I'll be awfully tired Saturday night. What do you say I come home Sunday morning?"

"No, Alex," insisted father Maclaren, "you've never been away from home before and these six days will seem like six years to me. Come Saturday night."

All week, young Maclaren thought about the trip he would have to make at night through the ravine. Saturday evening soon arrived. He packed his few belongings and walked to the edge of the canyon. As he stood staring into the inky darkness, he was scared. Tears welled up in his eyes. His heart told his head to move his feet on, but they remained motionless and still.

Suddenly, Alex heard footsteps. Just as he started to turn and run back toward Glasgow, out of the darkness came the grandest man on earth.

"Alex," the father said, "I've come to walk with you through the ravine."

As a great Presbyterian minister in later years, Dr. Maclaren

136

often recalled that ravine incident when discussing Psalm 23: ". . . I fear no evil, for thou [God] art with me."

I believe that God is the Master of space, time and predicaments of all sorts, shapes and sizes; therefore, you can count on Him to be your closest Companion through every situation. Rejoice! Take pride in God's presence with you.

As a result, you have good reason to *expect to work out the predicaments* when they happen. You, plus God, are a majority, and you can work out of the dilemma, but will you give 100 percent of yourself to make it through successfully? The people who work out predicaments are people who tap the mighty power of the Divine. That, in turn, enables *them* to work their way through every situation.

William James wrote, "If you care enough for a result, you will most certainly attain it. If you wish to be rich, you will be rich; if you wish to be learned, you will be learned; if you wish to be good, you will be good." Mix up this intense desire with honest effort and you can work out anything. Dr. James knew it; so did the great artist Leonardo da Vinci. "O Lord," da Vinci wrote in his notebook, "Thou givest us everything, at the price of an effort."

Henry Irving wanted to be an actor, but, as a critic testified, he had everything going against him. Young Irving could not speak and an actor must have sharp elocution. His walk was that of a sandlot cowboy: an actor has to have a graceful walk and, if he's a man, a manly walk. Furthermore, an actor cannot be afraid of people. He must look into their faces—eye to eye—but young Irving couldn't bear to look at anyone to whom he was talking. He either stared at the ceiling or the floor, or gazed out of a window, but never would he look at them.

Maybe Irving could take tidbit parts, but he even failed at that. Yet, his mind was made up, his heart was set, and he was willing to work hard. Only after years of tedious effort did he become the brilliant Shakespearean actor.

Effort! Work! Expect to *work* those circumstances out. Expect to *work* out those circumstances. Affirm your God-given power right now. "God and I can do it." Repeat that sentence ten times and mean it every time. Keep on assuring yourself with words like these, "I can do all things through Christ which strengtheneth me" (Philippians 4:13, KJV) and the unpredictable becomes a stairway to success.

PREPARING FOR THE UNPREDICTABLE

1. Resign yourself to the fact that a degree of unpredictability in life will be with you at all times.
2. Remember that a surprise can be turned into a success.
3. Be more concerned with the now of your life. (Tomorrow will be all right if today is.)
4. Look for good to come out of the unexpected in your life.
5. Develop a spirit that is grateful through surprises.
6. God is the Lord of the unpredictable, too; so consider Him as your nearest Friend.
7. And do everything you can to work through the surprises of life.

17.

—When There's a Death
in My Family?

It was about 3:30 in the morning when the phone next to my bed rang. "Reverend," began my young friend, Randy Fuhrman, on the other end of the line, "it's Dad. Dad just passed away."

I could hardly believe it.

"Randy, did you say that Ted passed away?"

"Yes, he had a heart attack and we're at the hospital emergency room."

Only eight hours before, I had laughed, joked and talked with forty-three-year-old Ted. He was a man whom I had grown to love as a jovial, outgoing sort of a person whom you couldn't help but like. He was an energetic churchman, a man on the upswing in life, a friend. The evening before, he had invited my wife and me to enjoy a dinner with them; but now, suddenly passed on!

How true are the words of Edmund Cooke.

> Death comes with a crawl,
> or comes with a pounce,
>   And whether he's slow or spry,
>   . . . you die.

Since death is one of life's inescapables, you have to consider what you can do when you lose a loved one or a close friend. There are several alternatives.

You can withdraw from life. *Withdrawal* is an inferior way of dealing with an acute interruption. It is to fight back by retreating. Maybe retreat is logical for military warfare, but never for life.

One of the most pitiful people I know is a young woman, who, in the face of a death, has withdrawn from life.

Bill and she had been married two years when Bill was drafted into the army. After training, he was sent to Viet Nam. Fear of his death became her constant companion, day and night. Sure enough, one morning, a captain rapped on the door and regretfully announced that Bill had been killed in action against the enemy.

The woman was hysterical for weeks; then she lapsed into prolonged sorrow, characterized by a severe withdrawal from life. "I don't want to live without Bill," she insisted. "People have no meaning to me now—no one." No one has been able to help her.

Although she still breathes, spiritually she is dead. She has no interest in her family or friends. Once an attractive person, she has let herself go. With a little effort, she could easily shape up again (mentally and physically) and win a deserving man; but, no, she has withdrawn from life. Retreat in the face of a challenge—that is what I call it.

An alternative is to continue in sorrow until it becomes *self-pity*. Resentment and bitterness parade close behind self-pity. This dangerous trio can creep into your life full force, and they will drag their emotional corruption with them.

Self-pity is feeling sorry for yourself. Carson McCullers, the famous American novelist, could have become a saint through self-pity—if self-pity were justified.

When she died, a critic described her career as a "vocation of pain." One leading authority and close observer said that her writings flowed from her own tortured life.

Still in her twenties, Mrs. McCullers suffered three strokes which left her a paralytic. Gradually, she commenced her writing again, but not without excruciating pain. Then her husband took his own life. "Sometimes," the brave woman was overheard to say, "I think God got Job and me mixed up. But Job never cursed God. Neither will I."

Take a sensible look at the uselessness of self-pity. It accomplishes nothing good. It adds nothing worthwhile. It is an illusion of the most terrifying sort. It puts you in a prison of misery. It is a sign without directions. It is a barrier to everything princely which your Heavenly Father aspires for you to be and do. It is a leech which sucks every ounce of creative energy from you.

Dr. David Abrahamsen, one of the outstanding counselors in our nation, said that a person of self-pity is unable to look at the whole picture of life. He thinks and acts only in terms of his own immediate feelings, his own inner world, thereby preventing himself from moving forward.

Self-pity isn't a gratifying alternative to take when there's a death in your family, but *grief* is a wholesome alternative. You can grieve successfully (which is a Christlike emotion) and thereby grow into a fuller person. Beyond a doubt, this alternative is the only one worth holding to. The question is, What can you do to grow through your grief into a richer life? First, remember the outstanding qualities of the loved one and let those qualities inspire you.

This is a victorious approach to the death of someone close to you. It is based on the fact that the deepest source for inspiration is not the negative aspects of a person's life, rather inspiration in its purest and most revitalizing form comes from the good side. This is the power of positive example which I have seen at work many times.

Joe Whipple of Covina, California, is an incurable optimist, a man to whom nothing is impossible. A friend of Joe's said one day, "I don't know how it happens. Some of the stuff he supports doesn't seem to be good business. He breaks a few of the accepted and normal laws, but he succeeds anyway. Even though it doesn't look like things will work out, they always do." His spiritual momentum and faith bring on victory.

Joe has worked hard on the church board for several years. The Valley Community Drive-In Church in San Dimas, California, has an endless drive to be a creative voice for Christianity in modern times. This takes a courageous board and congregation —men like Joe.

In one meeting where there was a great deal of discussion over programming, my friend Joe stood on his feet and said, "Gentlemen, these are bold programs which require a lot of faith and downright hard work. We have a big God, don't we? And He has given us healthy bodies to work, hasn't he? I think we ought to show some faith in Him and get on with the work. You can count on me 100 percent."

The positive example was effective immediately. Before the meeting was over, the decision had been made to move ahead with the imaginative programs, and every board member had committed himself to help us ministers believe, and work them through successfully.

The greatest and most positive Example ever on earth said that you are the salt of the earth and the light of the world (Matthew 5:13, 14 RSV). Be a positive example. Follow a positive example. Find the positive side of your close one who has passed away. The one gone might have had some weak points. If nothing else, you can say that the deceased wasn't as mean all the time as he was some of the time. Center your thoughts on the positive points. Your grieving will be successful.

Think of it in this way. Love is best inspired in others by love. Once in a while, you might be motivated to be courteous, patient and understanding by observing a discourteous, easily-provoked and short-tempered person. One teen-ager, after seeing such ridiculous displays by his dad, said, "No matter what else I do with myself, I'm going to be different from that!" Intelligent analysis leads us to conclude that if wrong will inspire good, how much more will good inspire good? Light gives light; love motivates love; wisdom spurs one on in quest of more wisdom. Then remember the best qualities of the loved one. They will serve as an example for you; they will inspire you to get out and do likewise. Those are the only memories worth storing in your mind anyway.

Live so that the thought of death doesn't embarrass you. *Live* is the word. Not exist! *Live!* Many people have been born into this world who have yet to really *live*. They eat, breathe, walk around, talk and work, but they are dead.

There was a religious organization which selected as its slogan, "Millions now living will never die." One of the officials in the group remarked, "True, but the modern tragedy is that millions now living are already dead and don't know it."

After attending a funeral service in Northeast Texas, I walked through that sleepy little cemetery near Annona and observed the inscriptions on the grave markers. Those words often shed some light on the life of the deceased, as this inscription did. "Born 1920. Died 1967. Lived 31 years." Out of forty-seven years on earth, the man had *lived* thirty-one years. To *live* so that death doesn't embarrass you, make every day the best day of your life. (You can do it!) Honor God, your Creator. Help people as best you can. Enjoy yourself. (You are a child of God!) Be happy with the simple ways of life. Never let your life overcomplicate living. Enjoy the common blessings, and keep enthusiasm for that which surrounds you.

H. G. Wells regretted letting life get overcomplicated, and for losing a sense of the spectacular in everyday realities. "There was a time," he said, "when my little soul shone and was uplifted at the starry enigma of the sky. All that has gone absolutely. Now I can go out and look at the stars as I look at the pattern of the wall-paper on a railway station waiting room."

Equally as important with *living* so that death doesn't embarrass you is the *attitude* that death is a friend to life rather than an enemy. The way a person acts when there is a death in his family often indicates that he thinks death is life's worst adversary.

It was my responsibility to tell a woman, for whom I have the highest regard, that her husband had a heart attack at work and died while being taken to the hospital. The news opened the gates to what doctors called a recessive tendency to be severely depressed. More important than the tragic news was her reaction to it. Reaction has more to do with a person's well-being in the face of calamitous circumstances than the circumstances themselves.

143

She has never pulled out of that acute depression. In those depressive thoughts, the woman has died a thousand deaths herself.

On the other hand, the death event is not an occasion for a carefree, jolly celebration. Such trivial treatment of the event creates a disrespectful atmosphere of the most nauseating type. It is an insult to the seriousness of the event. It invades the sacredness of death. Remember, however, that death of a close one can give an incentive for life; therefore, it is not to be feared. On one occasion, trusted advisors of Caesar suggested that he take better measures to protect his life. "He who lives in the fear of death," Caesar replied, "every moment feels its torture; I will die but once." In the old days, Pionius of Smyrna said that he was bent upon life, not death.

The Master was here for thirty-three years. As you read about Him in the Gospels, aren't you also impressed that He appreciated life? Don't you, too, see that He cherished life so much that each day was a fresh adventure to Him? It was in knowing that His years were limited here that He made each year count. Only then could He confidently pray on His cross, "Father, into thy hands I commit my spirit!" (Luke 23:46, RSV). Death certainly did not embarrass Jesus. It shouldn't embarrass you. It need not embarrass you.

To grow through grief, believe that physical death is a new beginning. This faith meets the demise of one close to you with certain victory.

Seldom have I seen this idea held to more tenaciously than by Oliver Randall. Ollie's body was twisted and wrecked by childhood polio, but his spirit was as bright and crisp as an April morning. He taught me a lesson I've never been able to forget.

"Pastor, I enjoy life. I really mean it! But when I die, there's going to be a new beginning!" His eyes sparkled like a thousand diamonds on a crystal lake.

Victor Hugo expressed it in these words: "When I go down to the grave, I can say, like so many others, 'I have finished my day's work.' Life is a thoroughfare. It closes on the twilight; it opens on the dawn." The vast universe is God's house. In this big house of His are many rooms. Death is but the foyer through which we pass from one room to another. Men are immortal and imperishable in their spirit. In passing from one room to another, the truth of Saint Paul is realized.

Death is swallowed up in victory.
O death, where is thy victory?
O death, where is thy sting?
(I Corinthians 15:55, RSV).

Sooner or later, I, too, will be a part of that transition we call death. If there is a public service, people will say in reference to David Ray, "Doesn't he look natural?"

But David Ray will not be there. There before their eyes will be the form in which he lived on earth, in which he tried to fully enjoy life and God and by which he hoped to help human beings; however, the spirit of David Ray will have already passed through the foyer into God's other room—with God.

Death is a new beginning! The end? A thousand times *no!*

"Surely goodness and mercy shall follow me all the days of my life; and I shall dwell in the house of the Lord for ever" (Psalm 23:6, RSV).

Believe it! Live it!

WHAT TO DO WHEN YOU LOSE A LOVED ONE

1. Seek divine guidance each day so that sudden develop-ments, like death of a loved one, will not wreck your plans.
2. Take every day as God's way of opening to you a fuller and happier life.
3. Assert your status as a child of God every day by living to the best of your ability. (Think of it as peak-efficiency living.)
4. Meet the unexpected in life with confidence and calmness.
5. Totally conduct yourself in such a way that if the day is your last, it is not a lost day.

18.

—When I'm Getting Old?

The man looked to be about fifty years of age. Those layers of oil and dirt caked on his uniform, and the charcoal grime covering his calloused hands, told me that he was a hardworking service-station attendant. Coming out to wait on me, he was a man of bouncy activity.

"Good afternoon, sir," he said as he approached the car. "Say," he went on, "you look like you need a little gas." (Even though it was a hot, energy-wilting day, I hoped he meant the car!) "I'd like to check under the hood. Are you in a hurry?" he asked.

I told him I needed to look at his map to find out the location of a family I wanted to visit.

"What street is it, sir?" he queried. "I might know and save you from looking."

I mentioned the street and he replied, "Oh, sure, go back to the traffic light, turn right, go two blocks, turn left, and it'll be the fourth street over."

With interest like that, he sure enough got my admiration. There was a lively tone in his voice; a youthful vitality leaped out from within him. He shuttled around the car whistling a merry tune, obviously delighted with his present state of life.

"My friend," I couldn't help saying, "You look to be fifty, but you have the spirit of thirty."

"I feel thirty," he exclaimed, "and I enjoy my work. I'm doing something for others here. I like people. I like to help people. I love my wife. I love my kids. And I love my church." In a final remark, he said, "Life means more to me than I can say."

Believe me, I drove out of that gas station a charged-up man! I had been feeling a little low when I pulled into that service station, but that man refueled a 1969 model car and a 1936 model David A. Ray!

You can be fifty years of age and still think thirty; you can be seventy and think thirty; you can be a centenarian and still in your spirit think thirty. If you maintain that glorious spirit of youthfulness, every year will be a better and happier year in your life, no matter how long you live.

Some of the wisest advice ever given came from the philosopher who said for us to live *all* of our lives. A tragic note left by a Los Angeles man who committed suicide, reads:

It seems that I have been around a long time. Too long. Much longer than the 26 years since my birth. Life hasn't meant much to me. You can say that at 26, I passed away of old age.

What perpetuates the spirit of thirty, no matter how many years a person has behind him? I believe that it has to do with the *aging psychology*. In the first place, the aging psychology is reflected more by your thinking than by the number of years you've lived. The *attitude* one holds, then, determines the age of his spirit.

What is the blessed secret of thousands who have remained young in their later years, and how is it done? Put into action the aging process which is a counter to the aging psychology. The aging process will cause a person to *grow* old; whereas, the aging psychology will *get* a person old. Thinking has a lot to do with it. *Attitude* sets the age of your spirit. Attitude is a mighty deterrent to the aging psychology.

A man asked me if he should start in business again, after two ventures had already failed. I replied that I could not answer such a question for anybody, but I could talk about some proven elements of success. Capital, know-how, market and market-potential are three ingredients.

"There's another component to success in any undertaking," I said. "It's attitude. Your attitude must be success bent."

I heard about a very perceptive business leader who told his key executives that attitudes are more important than aptitudes—

because attitudes affect the body. For the most part, the climate around us is created by our attitudes.

William James claimed that the greatest discovery of this generation is that human beings can alter their lives by altering their attitudes. Every person has his choice of becoming a fountain of youthful spirit or a spiritually- and emotionally-handicapped, mentally-restricted, age-burdened trickle of existence. You might say our attitudes determine our altitudes.

It has been a high note in my life to know Fred Bates. Fred is a dynamic Christian, a tireless church worker in my congregation and a topflight executive. Fred is Western Division Director for the widespread Eli Lilly Pharmaceutical Company. He has fifteen sales managers and hundreds of salesmen under him in the Western States, Alaska and Hawaii.

I dropped by to see Fred at his Pasadena office one afternoon.

"You're a man in contact with many men," I said. "You have the opportunity to rub shoulders in the business world with all kinds of problems and situations. Tell me, Fred," I said, hoping to learn something, "what is most important to the success of your drug salesmen?"

"There are sales techniques, knowledge of the products, desire to work, time spent on the job."

"All of these, but what is number one?"

Without hesitating, Fred replied in his deep, winsome Southern drawl, "*Attitude*—I mean *positive attitude*. The sales chart of a man reflects whether he has it or not. If things are going badly, I call in the man and talk to him about attitude. Get that straightened out," Fred claimed confidently, "and he'll make the sales."

In the whole of life, your attitude will set the pace (or destroy it).

I am not surprised at all, then, that the Bible says, "For as he thinketh in his heart, so is he" (Proverbs 23:7, KJV), nor that Jesus taught that from within the heart and mind of man comes wrong (Matthew 15:18), nor that Paul encouraged Christians to *think* no evil (I Corinthians 13:5, KJV), but there are more deterrents to that infernal aging psychology.

In addition to attitude, there is *hope*. The great Thomas Carlyle once said that man is based on hope. "He has no other possession but hope." It makes you into an incurable optimist who looks for bright skies, congenial work, true friends, a happy future and good health.

I heard one of the most respected doctors in America say that there is no medicine like hope, no incentive so great as hope and no tonic so powerful as the faith of something better tomorrow. Hope looks ahead with optimism and cheer. Always keep looking ahead with that.

At age sixty-five, a banker was forced to retire. Shortly, another bank asked him to organize a home loan department. At sixty-nine, the spirited man witnessed that the best is still ahead; he believed that the Lord gave him opportunity, strength, and courage to go on. That's the hopeful spirit of youthfulness, and God can get you going with it.

Hopelessness will make an aged man out of a young man. When Alfred Tennyson was told that Arthur Hallam, his closest friend, had died, he fell into deep despair. Life seemed futile and utterly hopeless. Had the great poet stayed in that state of hopelessness, his brilliant pen would have been stilled forever; but, as Tennyson verified, through faith in God and the future, he conquered hopelessness, and he rose to immortalize this hope in this tribute to his dear friend, *In Memoriam*. When you read that marvelous elegy again, notice the line which speaks of "the mighty hopes that make us men."

You will never stop the aging process (thank God, for that is a maturing process in which you grow old without getting old), but you must stop the aging psychology, which is to *get* old and miserable. Hope fosters the healthy aging process and counteracts the aging psychology. Here are some pointers on building up hope. Practice them and you'll *grow* old, but never *get* old.

1. Always be planning something good. (This will keep your mind turning. Stop thinking, and you'll rust out.)
2. Always look for something big to do. (This will keep your

hands busy. Many men have rotted away with boredom by sitting around doing nothing. Besides that, by sitting around the house, they get on their wives' nerves and drive them to the brink of insanity!)

3. Always look for good to happen. (Predict good. Don't be a doomsday prophet. Leave that for the less informed "old" people. By honestly looking for good to happen, you'll help bring it about.)

4. Always keep a gleam in your eye. (Never lose that faith that life is a great adventure.)

5. Always build the romance of life. (Love living. Think of it as a worthwhile gift from God. Life is really worth living at every age.)

6. Always learn everything you can. (You're not so old or so young that you cannot learn. You're not so smart that you cannot still learn a few things, and you're not so dumb that you can't learn. Continual learning will keep your mind awake and alert. If it goes to sleep, for all useful purposes, the body does, too.)

7. Always be thankful for your blessings. (A thankful spirit has a youthful tone about it.)

8. Remember, at the center of life is God. (You can find zesty living at any age as a blessing from Him.)

Another deterrent to the aging psychology is *enthusiasm*. I remember hearing a speaker say that years wrinkle the skin, but lack of enthusiasm wrinkles the soul. It has been demonstrated that lack of enthusiasm wrinkles the skin as well as the soul! A friend of mine compared a person with enthusiasm to a tea kettle. When he's up to his neck in hot water, he keeps on singing!

Actually, the root word for enthusiasm is *en* and *theos*, meaning "God in you."

Our church has been built on enthusiasm demonstrated through many people. When we make additions to the staff—whether ministers, secretaries, custodians, or gardeners—we gauge their enthusiasm. They've got to have it. When new board members and other officials are considered, their enthusiasm is of the most primary consideration. In a church, or any other sales organization (and the church is a sales organization), enthusiasm will get us over the toughest obstacles. *With it, we can succeed at everything. Without it, we'll not succeed at anything.*

At the age of forty, Bill Wagner had reached the high position of finance director for a billion-dollar company, but he decided to pursue a second career. Forty years of age is no problem to the man who has abundant enthusiasm, so, Bill energetically went on with his new plans. To start in the new business, he needed a sizeable loan.

"Can you point out any potential sources?" Bill asked me. "I'm going to get it, but I need to know where the possibilities are."

Most of the bankers I know are ones I owe, but I introduced him to them. Money was tight and interest rates were high, but Bill got the loan he needed—not from the first banker, or the second, or the third; but from the fourth. Enthusiasm pushed him through to success, and he would settle for no less than what he needed. The first three bankers offered loans in amounts less than his needs.

One of the six guiding principles in his life today is: pursue your goals with endless enthusiasm. Some call it ardor or zeal. It works. Bill's new business, a franchise, is off to one of the best starts in the company's remarkable history.

You can be certain that this enthusiasm generated by God will keep your spirit young. It will keep you dreaming, even the *impossible* dream. It will keep you driving ahead with successful persistence. It will keep you serving in the best interests of others. It will keep you looking at each day as an opportunity to really make your life count and to do something worthwhile. Oh, how mighty is enthusiasm! Especially when you add *faith* to it.

Realistically, *there is no enthusiasm of substantial character and force apart from faith.* This *faith* is another deterrent to the aging psychology. "All things are possible to him who believes," Jesus said (Mark 9:23 RSV).

Why is this faith so basic to your life and well-being? Because:

1. This faith is in God.
2. This faith is in yourself as a child of God.

3. This faith is in life as a good and wonderful gift of God.
4. This faith is a "doing" faith—active and working.

When Sir Harry Lauder's one and only son was killed in the war, he said to a close friend, "In a time like this there are three courses open to a man. He may give way to despair. . . . He may endeavor to drown his sorrow in drink. . . . Or he may turn to God."

As the years advance on you, there are several ways you can take them. One is resentment. (I don't like getting old; I don't want to get old.)

Another is worry. (Look at the bags under my eyes. They're there to stay! My skin is shriveling up. And this bursitis is killing me. You know, I don't get around like I used to.)

Still another is the ingrown self. (Oh, me, I'm getting too old to be useful. There's nothing I can do. I'm no account to anybody.)

You *can* maintain the youthful spirit; you *can* do anything. Faith makes it possible.

RIGHT ATTITUDES FOR GROWING OLD

1. Each day make God your Life-Partner. (Take His hand. Give Him yours. Visualize in your mind this as being done.)
2. At the beginning of each day, expect that day to be your best and thank God for the opportunities yet to come in it. (This will really get you going.)
3. Brighten the day by repeating faith-filling verses from the Bible. (Use an up-to-date translation because it is more easily understood.)
4. Pray, think, believe and act right attitudes and enthusiasm.
5. Keep your attitudes fresh and timely. (You're never so set in your ways that you cannot change and enjoy life.)
6. Build up a lively hope. (Fill yourself with it.)
7. Maintain enthusiasm for life and for what you're doing. (This will put excitement into every day.)
8. Keep in mind that the same power by which Jesus lived such a mighty life is your power to live today.

19.

—When It's Tough to Be Christian?

"I'm ready to give up," said the young businessman as he waited his turn in the barber shop. I didn't have the slightest idea what he was referring to until he explained.

"It's no use trying to live a clean, conscientious life in these business circles. People sometimes are vicious, downright cruel, and double-dealing. The best thing to do is to deaden your conscience, grit your teeth and stiffen up your will against good. Get mean, and run over anybody who gets in your way. You know, Reverend, it's tough to be Christian on Wilshire Boulevard."

Wilshire Boulevard defined his business world.

Robert Browning wrote in *Easter Day*, "How very hard it is to be A Christian!" But just how difficult is it? Is it really tough?

As another businessman and I mulled over these questions one day, he reached inside his coat pocket and pulled out a folder of cards, about 2 by 3 inches in size.

"My instant-inspiration pack," he grinned. Written on those cards were inspirational verses for happy living—from the Bible. "When I feel like reaching for a pack, this is the pack I come up with," he spoke confidently. "Now, let's see. The great Example said something about how tough it is to be Christian. Here it is."

Come to me, all who are (weary and overburdened), and I will give you rest. (Put on) my yoke and learn from me . . . you will find rest for your souls. For my yoke is easy and (the weight of my yoke) is right (for you)" (Matthew 11:28-30). [Sic]

"That's quite a statement, isn't it?" he said. I thought it over. In it the Master outlines a divine law, then fires it up with a torch of encouragement. The law isn't complicated, nor is it bloated with superfluous language. You and I can understand it, accept it and live by it. In common terms, the law is: Come to God, learn His way for your life and you will find peace within—peace of soul and mind for living today. Many people are troubled on the inside and need the vital peace which this law brings.

While flying across the country, I met a classic illustration of modern-man-in-conflict. The inner struggle had etched itself across his troubled face. His demeanor indicated the strife—nervous, jittery and restless.

"What's your business?" he asked.

"Oh, I'm a salesman," I answered.

"Why, so am I," he said. "At least, I'm supposed to be—was one, anyway."

"What's your line?" he asked.

"Pardon me," I muttered. "What did you say?"

"What's your line?" he repeated, "Your product?"

"Oh, yes—well, I'm a salesman for God. What's yours?"

"Carpet and floor coverings. Salesman for God? What d'ya mean?"

"I sell the greatest system of ideas for personal happiness, successful living and joyful relationships this world has ever known. My product has no peers."

Just about the time he began to look as if he'd like to apply for a job with the company I work for, I said, "I'm a minister. I sell Christianity."

After telling him that, I listened as he said, "Then you've got peace in your inventory, and I sure need some of it."

"Yes," I assured, "there is peace in our inventory, and plenty of it."

"Lend me your ear," commented the man. "I've botched up three big deals in a row. Does the peace you market gear a man to handle such revolting developments?"

"Indeed it does. Poise and power are its trademark."

Come, Learn, Find: that is the law of methods and results.

Come by prayer. Come believing. Come in reliance upon Him. Learn from Christ's life. Take on His spirit of love, His outlook of optimism, His boundless enthusiasm, His driving purpose in life to be a people-lifter and His devotion to God. Learn more every day. Keep the wheels of spiritual intellect turning. They rust when they sit still. You will find peace inside by coming and learning. That is God's law! Unchangeable and certain!

You can Come, you can Learn, you can Find *whoever* you are —rich or poor, mighty or minute, young or old, kings or commoners, black or white, large or small, known or unknown.

You can Come, you can Learn, you can Find *wherever* you are: on Wilshire Boulevard, on Fifth Avenue, in the classroom, on the campus, in the ghetto, in the city, in the village, on the rolling hills, in the flowing farmlands, on the open plains, in the woodlands, on the assembly line, in the home, on vacation, on the battlefield, at the conference table, sailing the seas, soaring the spacious skyways, or on the sandy beach front. *Wherever* . . . yes, even on the beach.

One of the organizations which specializes in taking God to the beach front has headquarters only a few miles from where I live. It is called Campus Crusade for Christ. Working in it are Christians of all denominations. Under the direction of highly-trained and enthusiastic Christians, thousands of collegians flock to the beaches of this land and confront people, especially other college students, with this great law.

California beaches teem with tens of thousands of funseeking collegians on Eastern vacation. Among them you will find these happy Christians from Campus Crusade. There is Marilyn Campbell, a staff member for the Crusade, and Portia Campbell is there, too, along with several other young people from my congregation. They are helping to change their world by giving a law that changes people from the inside out. Portia told me about one experience she had down at Newport Beach.

"I walked over to this couple. They had been drinking some, but not very much. I was sure," Portia commented, "that I had found a need which could be filled by God working through me. I asked their names."

"I'm Bob. My girl here is Barbara."

"Hi, Bob and Barbara. I'm Portia from Whittier College. What's your school?"

"Stanford," Bob answered.

It didn't take long to get their attention. Portia is a very attractive young woman, which Bob noticed right away. So did Barbara, I am certain! But with her winsome looks, Portia has personality plus and a happy, victorious spirit, and she has a marvelous religious experience to match.

Portia shared a few questions through which she discovered that Bob and Barbara weren't up on religion. "Church stuff isn't our bag," he claimed. Barbara added that the last time she went to church (which was more than two years back), the affair was so boring that she yawned halfway through the service. "Minister didn't say much," she commented.

Such statements did not stop Portia. She quickly replied. "But if you can have religion that puts power for living into you, wouldn't you want it?"

"Maybe," Bob said.

"And if that religion puts happiness in you and helps you to have fun at living, wouldn't it be worthwhile?"

"Yes," they nodded.

"Then you want Jesus Christ and His way for life," Portia suggested. And there at the edge of the great Pacific Ocean, the Stanford couple made a genuine commitment to God. They came; they found; they began to learn.

Dr. Jonathan Edwards, a pioneer minister, educator and philosopher referred to it as a leveler. "There is no leveler like Christianity," he said, "but it levels by lifting all who receive it to the lofty table-land of a true character and of undying hope. . . ."

To paraphrase some wonderful words of the Peace Maker, "You'll not find the coming and learning tough, nor will you find the rest hard to take. As a matter of fact, the life you can live by coming and learning will be easy." What is this matter about easy living? My usage of *easy* refers to comfortable, useful, profitable, agreeable and good living. Don't mistake it for softy, sudsy, seepy living. Christianity is the way for red-blooded people!

This *living begins within you*. External living is, for the most part, the projection of internal thoughts and ideas. What is inside determines what is outside. If Christianity is tough to you, it is tough from the inside out. It is hard for anyone *whose heart is not in it*.

There was a young man who had the promise of becoming the greatest schoolboy high jumper in state history, but he couldn't seem to go over a certain height. The coach knew that the boy could jump far above that mark, but he wanted the young man to know it. One day, the fellow came to his mentor.

"Coach," he asked, "what's the trouble? I'm trying so very hard, but I don't go over five feet eight inches?"

The coach showed some great insight for living, as well as accomplishment on the track field, when he replied, "Tom, if you want your body to go over five feet eight inches, you've got to send your heart first."

Heart first is the seasoning for much of life's ease. I like to think of my father as one of the finest self-trained, home gardeners anywhere. A man asked me how it is that Mr. Ray, at retirement age, gets so much done and does it so well. "First," I said, "his heart is in it."

The key to happiness with your work, whether it be in a machine shop or a carpeted executive suite, will be found basically in the heart. Where is your heart? That means desire! "For where your treasure is, there will your heart be also," Jesus once said.

Being Christian is also difficult for *anyone who has hate in his mind*. Hate has many arms. One of them is selfishness. The *yoke* the Master talks about is a symbol of service.

Service, helping others, is the reverse of selfishness, yet it achieves the ends for which people are selfish. Human beings want for themselves without regard for others. That is selfishness, but it is by regarding others that self is truly lifted.

"Sickness and self-centeredness go hand in hand," said a physician in Glendora, California to a gathering of ministers. He discussed therapy for a group of retired, sickly men and women.

The doctor suggested that the women make clothing for little children in an orphanage nearby. The prescription for the men included a challenge to repair used toys which had been donated to the Salvation Army to distribute to less fortunate boys and girls at Christmastime. The women were quite able to make the clothes, and they knew how to make them. The men were very capable of taking those old toys and putting them in a condition to make many boys and girls happy at Christmas; yet, the men and women refused. Later they changed their minds and accepted. "From the day the women began to sew those clothes for the orphans and the men to repair those toys for the children," the doctor reported, "recovery from their ills was remarkably noticeable." Selfishness had become a perpetuator of their sicknesses.

The doctor closed his speech by saying that in a real and basic sense, it is in serving that you are served; in dying (to the bad or wrong) that you live; in forgiving that you are forgiven; in giving that you are given to; and in giving that you get.

Hate, however, blocks God's law for graceful and healthy living. The hate-filled mind is infected, and it restricts the realization of the Almighty's law for living. In fact, hate, in any of its forms, nullifies the law as far as that law has any practical effect on a person.

Drain out hate and its children—Hostility, Resentment, Grudges, Self-Pity and that old parasite, the I-can't attitude. A daily drain time can be vital to a person's life. Make some time everyday, near its close, during which you, with God's help, flush out these mental and spiritual culprits. Mention them individually, those that have slipped into your mind during the day. Recount the cause for them, then dismiss them. Let them go. If your feelings are against another person, "God bless" that person. Say it in your prayers. Mean it. No one can hold hate for long toward somebody he is "God blessing." Put a finality to the hate feelings by saying, "Lord, I am letting them go into your hands. Now." Recount your blessings. Thank God for them. You get the love spirit in this way.

Living a successful Christian life is hard for anyone who has the *tough-life complex*. Some people who say they are living the great life keep complaining about it. They puncture almost every step with grumblings.

Life and religion for some people are little more than foaming, moaning and groaning, but you can take heart in this fact. That kind of religion didn't start with Jesus, and the Galilean had the greatest antipathy for it. This kind of religion starts in the thoughts. Christianity is hard for anybody who starts thinking it is hard.

A thought is a word and deed in construction. It's a word yet to be said and a deed still to be done. String thoughts together and you have a system of thinking. For that reason, thoughts are elementary to your life. When you think long enough, you start believing what you think; then what you think and believe, you project out into reality.

Actualized retreat, organized defeat, systematized failure and realized calamity don't take form and substance until they are jelled in your *thinking*. Along the same lines, *Christianity is made hard for oneself, by oneself, within oneself*. Oh, the magic of that thought power within you!

The flow of black gold has taken a sizeable number of farm folk in Texas from eking out a meager hand-to-mouth existence to more comfortable living. Two of those wonderful people were Jess and Mattie. Jess' father and grandfather had worked the one hundred sixty acres of farmland before him, but no one had made any money doing it. The bare necessities of life were all they could afford.

One day, an engineer from one of the oil companies came by to tell Jess that they were sure a big lake of liquid money was under his land. A contract was signed, drilling began and the biggest oil strike in that region was made. "And to think" said Jess in a reflective mood, "it was within this ground all that time—in Papa's day, and in Grandpapa's time, too."

Within you is the golden power for agreeable and useful Christianity. Christianity can be tough, but thank God, there are some ways to get rid of that complex. If religion is hard to you, you can shed that unnatural complex.

159

STEPS TO AGREEABLE AND USEFUL CHRISTIANITY

1. Receive the words of Jesus at face value.
2. Receive those words at full value.
3. Through prayer to God, condition your thinking process from one of defeat and difficulty to one of victory and ease.
4. Start believing that you can live as Jesus did.
5. Go out today and do something which Jesus did.
6. Each day, deliberately do something which Christ Himself did during His life here.
7. Begin thanking God for the ease with which you are able to enjoy Him and life.